Impacting
the City

Impacting the City

Martin Scott
with
Mike Love and Sue Sinclair

Sovereign World

Sovereign World Ltd
PO Box 777
Tonbridge
Kent TN11 0ZS
England

ISBN 1-85240-400-0

The publishers aim to produce books which will help to extend and build up
the Kingdom of God. We do not necessarily agree with every view expressed
by the author, or with every interpretation of Scripture expressed. We expect
each reader to make his/her judgement in the light of their own
understanding of God's Word and in an attitude of Christian love and
fellowship.

Cover design by CCD, www.ccdgroup.co.uk
Typeset by CRB Associates, Reepham, Norfolk
Printed in the United States of America

Dedicated to
Micha and Anette Siebeneich.

Contents

Preface

Since mid 1998 I have had the privilege of partnering with so many people through the work of Sowing Seeds for Revival in numerous cities in the UK, and more latterly within different nations in mainland Europe, as well as a number of cities in the US, particularly on the West Coast. As the journey has continued, I have gleaned fresh approaches through this interaction with different people in the various situations. This book is largely the fruit of that journey. Ideas that I think are original to me are probably not, for I am sure that someone will have seeded virtually every concept of value in this book with sharper insights than my own. If there are concepts within the chapters I have written that need some radical adjustment, sadly those might well be original!

In the previous book, *Gaining Ground*,[1] the main focus was related to the development of strategic prayer, although it also touched on new shapes for church, and how to engage with the community outside the church structures. In this book I am looking to take these concepts further, seeking to explore the very real possibility of reaching a city through developing a fourfold approach. This fourfold approach can be summarized under four headings: the need for those carrying responsibility within the pastoral realm of the Body of Christ to find a unity together; the necessity of believers to stand through every sphere in our cities; the desire for multi-level prayer to be developed; and the development of the prophetic watchpeople in the city so that the voice of God is being heard through all that is taking place. If these elements are increasingly in place, I believe that there will be a consistent call for the presence of God, and the possibility of something that might be described as a city eldership coming into place. These are the concepts that will be developed through this book, and Chapter 2 will outline the fourfold approach in more detail. (I originally was describing the process as being threefold: church leaders, saints in the spheres and multi-level prayer, but in interaction with a team I work with, Building Together, I have come to see that it is helpful to separate the ministry of the watchperson from that of prayer. As always there are no hard lines between the categories, but for the purpose of analysis it is necessary to bring in distinctions: in life all four categories have to flow together.)

The final chapters are devoted to the concept of there being a limited number of city-types. This is intended to help us understand the nature of our particular city so that we will be better equipped to develop appropriate strategies for obtaining a breakthrough. In writing on the city gifts my hope is that this will stimulate further research as what is contained here in this book is certainly not the final word on the subject.

I am very grateful to Mike Love for agreeing to write Chapters 3 – 5 that deal with the development of the church in the city and how there can be a healthy relationship across the city, both inside but particularly beyond the congregation. I am especially thankful not only because his contribution has proved to be an immense practical help, but also because I believe he is much more qualified to write about such issues than I am. Over the past few years I have been enormously provoked by Mike, and I know that his chapters will be read with great interest.

Sue Sinclair also contributes a chapter that tells the story of the development of prayer on Merseyside (Chapter 7). She has been very involved with this and she is a great encouragement to me personally. What is taking place there is not perfect, but it is a parable that we can learn from. Sue is someone who has taken the call of God seriously and has seen significant results as she, with others, has pursued the prayer agenda.

The concept of there being a limited number of city-types was originally sparked in me through the teaching of Arthur Burke. Although, through experience, I was beginning to see how some cities resembled each other, I do not think I would have followed this through to the extent I have without his teaching input.

I dedicate this book to Micha and Anette and my many friends in Germany who have welcomed me to their land. Europe so needs a spiritually strong Germany.

Finally, I trust you will enjoy this read as much as I have enjoyed putting the book together. I hope, though, that you find it an easier read than I did a write!

Note

1. *Gaining Ground: Prayer Strategies for Transforming Your Community* (Baker House, 2004) became the title for the book once it was published in the US; in the UK it was originally published as *Sowing Seeds for Revival* (Sovereign World, 2001).

Chapter 1

A Time for Fulfillments

If we are not prepared for the hard work of ploughing, any hope we had of reaping will prove to have been false, for as Proverbs 20:4 says,

"A sluggard does not plough in season;
so at harvest time he looks but finds nothing."

We all wish to harvest, but if we are not prepared to work hard at the level of preparation (ploughing and sowing) we will find ourselves being very disappointed. Just before I began to travel with prayer teams in June 1998, a church leader asked me how long I envisaged traveling in that capacity. I replied that I anticipated I would need to do so for at least four to six years even to begin to scratch the surface. (I write these words toward the end of my sixth year and do believe that we are now beginning to see fruit as a result.) The look on his face told me he was hoping I would say "a few months" so that we might all be able to rest back and experience the presence of revival in the nation by then. He was hoping that all our hard work would be over, as people in significant numbers would be responding to salvation. Revival – the answer to all our problems! What a wonderful thought, but I also suspect a major myth!

There seems to me to be only two legitimate "finishing lines" that are given to the church in Scripture – the return of Jesus and the taking of the gospel to the ends of the earth. Indeed, it is likely that these two finishing lines will prove to be one and the same. Certainly Scripture does not lead us to expect that with just a little more effort revival will come, thus ending all our problems! No, hard work, difficulties and setbacks will be with us till He returns. Thank God, Scripture is considerably more realistic than we are. And thank God that the Scriptures are there to fill us with the faith we need to believe God for the turning of cities and also nations.

We find ourselves alive at a time of significant shift in Western culture. This mega-shift is affecting every expression of that culture, including church. Death is around us; the end of an era is visible. For those with hope, though, this can also herald the beginning of a new era for death can once again yield to new life. A new expression of church is looking to burst through the dust of death that currently covers our culture. New life, when it appears, will express itself in ways that are both continuous and discontinuous with what has gone on previously. So, in our current setting the church that is coming to birth will manifest some of what has gone before – it will be recognizable – but it will also appear with many new aspects. The future of church will almost certainly be more diverse than ever, and yet the possibility of a deeper level of unity will be more within our grasp than before.

I advocate that we do not yield to the quick-fix mentality of "revival as the answer for all problems," and that we also embrace this wider framework that the Western church is now at the end (and beginning) of an era. Those factors indicate that our task of effectively reaching our generation has to be a considered one. Thus far what I have written could well be interpreted as if I am pessimistic about our potential for success. However, given the chapter title as "A Time for Fulfillments," I hope it will become clear that far from being pessimistic I am, in fact, optimistic and (I trust) realistic.

In spite of death, my convictions are that we are in a time of fulfillment. Provided we engage with whatever hard work proves necessary to fulfill our task, we can genuinely anticipate an experience of revival that will not disappoint. The very word "revival" creates a diversity of images and I think it is only fair that I first expand on how I understand the concept in our culture.

Revival: what do we mean?

The word "revival" is a hard one to give definition to. At one level it is not a biblical concept, for if the word is to have any meaning at all it is only applicable to a church that has fallen asleep (or died). Only such a church needs reviving. Surely God never intended the church to sleep, and "revival" language can be dangerous for two reasons: it can suggest that a revival dynamic is abnormal and that such abnormality solves all ills.

Yet the word is applicable in the sense that the church, as we experience it, continually needs reviving. And provided we understand that God desires the church to rise again to the challenge of incarnating the life of Jesus within our culture, it is not an inappropriate term. So long as we do not fall into the "revival-cures-all-ills" trap, it seems appropriate to me to use the term "revival" as a statement of our hope.

I do believe revival is coming – and in measure is already here in many places – but I am agnostic as to how it will be expressed. I am sure there will be some great inbreakings of the Spirit, for that typifies the unpredictability of the wind of God (John 3:8), but, in all honesty, my overall hope is that we see the church rise from her sleep and grow increasingly into the fulfillment of her call. Sudden increases might well be more exciting, but an experience of steady growth might well prove to be healthier than a sudden explosion of the life of God. Statistically it has been suggested that the early church grew at some 40 per cent per decade virtually every decade for some 300 years – definite steady growth and, dare I suggest it, truly revival growth. I also consider that steady growth will more likely deal with our wrongly placed desire for God to do for us what He has already challenged us to do. He asks that we work out what He has worked in us; that we grapple with the suffering of creation and so come through to a place of humble stewardship. Hence, steady and consistent growth should indeed prove to be healthier.

If God comes to accelerate things dramatically, and He most surely will, so well and good but, if not, then we need to know what it is we are to get on with, and to set in place. Perhaps there has never been a greater opportunity to demonstrate the manifold wisdom of God, not only to the heavenly powers, but also to those around us. God does have a "meta-narrative" that He is telling, for He is the beginning and the end, and that story must be told and re-told in every generation through a myriad of cameos.

For that story to be told we, as part of the Body of Christ, will need to connect with our community. As a connection is made with the community, the church becomes a redemptive body and enables the setting (people and geography) to begin to connect with the amazing redemptive story that runs from creation to consummation. If the church can embrace the truth that God has called her to be a body of destiny, then seeds of destiny can be sowed into the wider community. The story to be told, then, is not our story but His. The challenge facing any church leadership is to flow in such a way that any sub-vision that they are proposing is not centralized in a controlling fashion, but is ready to give way to the wonderful transformation message of the gospel. Too often leaders have developed a vision that is centered in on the growth of the church numerically and its activities – the end result being one of stifling the bigger vision of the church being redemptive in and through all of creation. Any vision developed at a church level can only be temporary. It continually has to die in order that Jesus becomes center stage in God's meta-narrative that is directed by the Spirit.

Revival then, for me, both speaks of the awakening of the church to fulfill her creation mandate and also of great inbreakings of the Spirit, so that through the church the presence of the future is manifest for any society to view.

Fulfillments

Into the context I have outlined above I want to speak of hope, of a season of fulfillments that is here before us in the Western church. Yet, before writing about fulfillments, let me also under-line that the pathway to any fulfillment will always include a death experience. There is no successful fulfillment without death. The path from promise to fulfillment must travel by way of the cross.

However, enough realism for now! In Easter of 1991 I was in South Africa and over a period of days a vision began to take shape. I wrote down, under a number of headings, the things I believed were going to take place. I will give the headlines below and then put a little more substance to them as I explain how I currently understand the various aspects.

(Just before giving the headlines it is worth noting at this stage that I used to think "UK" whereas now I think "Europe," so the scope of the vision is the European church. Later, I will make a comment as to why I see the North American continent also as "European.")

▶ *A new type of church was to rise*

In my notes I wrote down "Apostolic Church." This type of church would have great authority over a region. It would be as if that region had opened up spiritually and, even if one traveled some fifty miles from that place, the atmosphere elsewhere might still be closed. The contrast was very marked. Within the context of apostolic church I saw that there would be a great release of signs and wonders.

▶ *Different ages released*

A great youth movement was coming. These young people would be sold out and ready to go at the Lord's command. A number of these young people would not live the majority of their lives in the UK, but would relocate to other European cities, thus helping to form the end of a bridge, with the result that many cities became inter-connected.

Corresponding to this youth movement there would also be a movement among those aged approximately fifty-five and above. Some of those would have been on the edge of church but would find themselves catapulted into the heart of God's action plan; others simply stepped into something new, so that their latter years proved to be more fruitful than all their former ones put together. A number of these people took early retirement, with not a few living out the remainder of their lives in nations other than the nation of their birth.

▶ Business and transformation

I saw business people finding one another, and in particular finding one another internationally. Through their relationships they began to spark each other to such an extent that the day came when they would travel to nations that were under bondage through debt and poverty. They would gain entrance to those in power and let them know that they had come from God, but they did not come to simply hand out finances but to help with the reshaping of the nation. The poverty of certain nations was broken in a short period of time, and there was a level of unprecedented fruitfulness for the gospel.

▶ An arts revival

Finally, the arts were impacted. Something more than "Christian drama" broke loose. The largest auditoriums in Europe were taken, and there was a revival of the arts in the streets. The latter opened up the wells of creativity; the former brought the color of God to the public arena.

Some comments on the vision

In 1991 I had only one framework for the concept of "apostolic church." I thought that such a church would be where a local church – similar to "my" one! – would grow to unprecedented levels and make a major impact on the spiritual atmosphere, as well as impressing everyone around!! Given that my church would be one of them, that was wonderful as I was in it!

However, I have become convinced that a big church is not what is going to do the job. Or, perhaps more accurately, a big "local" church is not going to do it. However, if we could actually see and live from the revelation that there is a much larger church across our locality than our local church, then there is real hope that larger church will fulfill this vision. In other words, I now see church in the city or across the region as that Body that the Lord is raising up, or "reviving," to a level of apostolic authority. Leadership for this new expression of church will inevitably be different from the structures that have led what we have called "local church." Indeed, some of the basic relational units might be smaller than anticipated, but the true bond of unity will be greater than before so that the church in the locality will truly begin to rise with an apostolic mantle.

Even many successful local churches are going to find themselves entering major transition. Unless there is an embracing of new relationships, in response to John 17, it will not be possible to rise up to participate in this new apostolic dimension. Inevitably, there will have to be major redefinitions given to the words "apostle" and "apostolic." Those who were apostolic in one era of church life might not automatically be apostolic in the next phase of development. The apostolic ministry is foundational, and in every move of God there will be apostles raised up to lay foundations for the expression of church coming out of that particular move.

There is a generation that is rising that will bring us into a level of fulfillment that has eluded us thus far. Youth and those who are not youth (I can't refer to those over fifty-five as elderly) are together that rising generation. All who are prepared to rise as part of what the Lord is doing will be the rising generation, regardless of age, for God is not the God of age. If what is rising is not marked by a certain age, it will however be marked by certain characteristics of the Spirit. Although the rising generation is not primarily to do with age, it also needs to be stated that, if we do not see the youth touched in what is coming, we will have fallen drastically short of a revival movement that is in the heart of God. So, although it will not simply be youth that rise, it is necessary that a major part of what is coming be expressed through the younger generation.

The impacting of the business and arts arenas will be vital if we are to see a transformation that goes beyond our churches and touches our cities and nations. I cannot speak into these areas with any great expertise, but these spheres of activity will be addressed at some level in the context of this book. The saints are getting ready for their release and empowerment, and we are gladly having to plan for the church to be placed in the context where God always desired it to be: the world. A church truly gathered under one heavenly head is one that is placed in and through all of creation.

I trust by now that you will begin to see where this book is aiming. I believe we need our faith to be stirred for new expressions while keeping our feet firmly planted on terra firma. We need to be people of prayer and of hard work. We need to love the church, but refuse to be held captive by concepts from a former era.

So, from my perspective revival is necessary to bring the church back to a level that God intended. This is an ongoing issue and, inasmuch as the church is already being re-aligned with the purposes of God, this reviving is already present among us in measure. We are now coming into a season of fulfillments, when much of what was prophesied into the nations, churches and individuals at the end of the 1980s and beginning of the 1990s will find fulfillment. Whenever prophecies are given they have to be received and waited on for their fulfillment, and I believe now is the time for fulfillments increasingly to take place.

If this is so, we can also expect a few changes. When we move into fulfillments our experience will be different to what it was in the days of promise. One of the main aspects that we can expect is that prophetic intercession will begin to make room for apostolic declarations. I do not mean by this that there will be no more prophetic intercession, but that we will increasingly come to a time when what has been travailed over will be established. As this begins to happen the church will stand in a new place and declare what God has established.

Before, however, touching on these apostolic declarations there is the need for a brief explanation of what I mean by the term "prophetic intercession." I am using this term to cover every aspect of intercession (including prayer but not simply referring to prayer exclusively) that seeks to address the gap between what is and what should be. Historical sin has caused great divisions, like fissures in the ground. A good example of historical sin is that of the "bloodguilt" that has been on the nation of Germany (and I certainly don't want to give the impression here that there is no bloodguilt on the UK for the wars that devastated Europe, in fact I believe that Germany is currently cleaner than England is over these issues). Over years many have stood in the gap on this issue and many actions have been implemented (prophetic intercession), with the result that today the bloodguilt has been removed from the nation. I, following the lead of others, have been privileged to stand on a new platform in Germany – a platform that is free from past bloodguilt. Truly that guilt has been removed. God really does forgive sin; repentance does turn a nation to God.

Prophetic intercession has created a platform for increasing apostolic declarations, where the effects of the sin can be proclaimed as over. Or, using other words, apostolic declaration is where what is declared on earth through the church is made effective in the heavens (Matthew 18:18). This is not a technique but a level to which the Lord wishes to take the church in order that the prophetic intercession of recent years will, indeed, bear much fruit.

At the beginning of 2002 I was able to take a prayer team to the northern part of France. I was so overwhelmed by the heaviness that was descending that I pressed in for a few days to try and understand what was going on. The Lord said that I was to declare that the spirit of grief had been broken off the nation and that the church was now to stand in that new position. The church in the nation is called by God to be a prophetic sign by leading the way and demonstrating that true *joie de vivre* comes from the Spirit of God. The nation is destined to be a joyous nation of abandoned lovers and worshipers, but the blood shed on French soil had called for a spirit of grief. Through intercession these things can be broken and then the church has to rise up and make a bold apostolic declaration.

What has been happening across Europe is that prophetic

intercession, led in the main by faceless people, has begun to break through. Old strongholds are weakening, and this is making room for something new to rise up – an apostolic type church across cities, regions and even nations that will begin to make declarations. In so doing, a new order in the heavens will open over cities and even over whole nations. Such an apostolic church will only be birthed out of intercession and will manifest in a true spirit of unity.

The United Kingdom and Europe

If the UK church is to break through it is vital that we embrace our European identity. In spite of our isolation we have a history that binds us together. We are of the same stock and we are being called to play our part in the reforming of a continent. By using the word "reforming" I am making a deliberate choice. We are being called to re-form, to put together shapes that are calling for God to fill them. (In Genesis 1, we read that this was how God first responded to a creation that was without form and empty – He made shapes or forms that He then later filled.) The Lord is encouraging us to pray and work for a manifestation of church across Europe that will cause there to be an even greater shake-up than was caused at the time of the former Reformation.

There are fears in the UK (as well as in other European nations) about a united Europe. This is understandable both from a political and spiritual perspective. However, if the church in the UK does not engage with the reshaping of a spiritual unity within the church in Europe, and make a choice to share the burden of our corporate guilt, we will have no one to blame but ourselves when a demonic and domineering Europe rises up. Dare I suggest that the Lord is calling for a united Europe – at the level of the Body of Christ, and that the enemy wants to counterfeit this with an oppressive and even persecuting structure.

If through listening to negative voices about Europe, the UK church responds by withdrawing, then those voices will prove to be self-fulfilling prophetic voices. If however, the church rises up in prayer and love, then a new Europe could be formed. The gospel must again shape up the continent that God graced for so long as a mission-sending continent, and for that to happen the UK church must respond by embracing her European identity and destiny.

John the Baptist

One final biblical analogy will, I believe, help us. I was present in a city where the unity among church leaders is as significant and as deep as I have seen anywhere. The unity could not be described as superficial for the pastors have wept with each other, asking for forgiveness, the one of the other. They asked me if they should see themselves as a "city eldership." (I always find the answer given in those situations very educational, as the Holy Spirit loves to respond to our honest, humble search after truth.) Here was a situation that was as close as I had seen to that of a city eldership, but surprisingly I found myself saying the following:

> "You are not to see yourselves as a city eldership, but you are to live, pray and exist with the burden and mandate to release a city eldership. When it comes through some of you might be part of it, some might not. However, if you do not live with the responsibility of producing a city eldership, then it might not arise; also if you were to see yourselves at this time to be that city eldership you will actually prevent it from fully rising."

In other words, their task was to be that of intercession, of standing prophetically for what was coming, and of calling for it. Their task was not to make claims for themselves, or to see themselves as what was coming. I then went on to say that they were to be like John the Baptist, who faced a similar line of questioning in John 1. So, as I close this chapter, let's take a brief look at the dialogue in that chapter, and in particular John's response.

Who are you?

The representatives of the Jewish Temple authorities came to John to ask him to state who he was. In doing so, they gave him some alternatives. With each option presented he responded with a denial. Jesus was clearly the fulfillment of the first option presented ("Are you the Messiah?"). John also denies that he is the fulfillment of the last option ("Are you the Prophet?"). He was not the Prophet, for it was Jesus who truly was the Prophet like Moses (Deuteronomy 18:15–17). It is, however, the middle option in John 1:21 that they gave to John (*"Are you Elijah?"*) that we know to be most accurate. For Jesus Himself said that John was, indeed, the Elijah that had been promised (see, for example, Matthew 11:14 for Jesus' comments, and Malachi 4:5–6 for the promise concerning Elijah).

Why, then, does John deny this identification? It is most unlikely that John did not self-consciously see himself as the fulfillment of the Elijah prophecy. I suggest that it would have been very difficult for John to do what he did, had he not seen himself as carrying the spirit of Elijah. Also, given that John's father, Zechariah, had been told explicitly by Gabriel of John's identity, it seems most unlikely that this identity was kept from him. So, I suggest that John knew very well that he was, indeed, the person destined to stand in the anointing of Elijah.

Why then the denial? Two reasons. First, Jesus had said that John was Elijah *if* the people were able to receive it. The fact that they were asking the question indicated that they were not, in reality, receiving him as Elijah. So his answer to the question "Are you Elijah?" is, in effect, "No, I am not – at least I am not Elijah *to you*." Those sent from heaven only fully succeed in their mission when they are received as ones sent.

The second factor, though, is that John was so focused on what was to come that he could not be diverted to discuss his own identity. When forced, he described himself simply in relation to what he was called to do. He was a voice, crying out in the wilderness. If he did not stand in the gap until he saw who was to come established, he would fail. What positive purpose could possibly result from debating who he was? If he fulfilled his task, then indeed it could be said that he was Elijah, but not before. And if he did fulfil his task, then it was never about him anyway, but about the one who was to come.

It is this attitude that must permeate all current activities. We are to be voices that intercede for what is to come. We are to take ourselves so seriously that we are willing to live and die for what is to come. We, however, realize that what is to come is so much greater than we are that we cannot raise ourselves up with great titles. So, we take what we are called to do very seriously, but can never view ourselves with intrinsic importance.

The great call from the heart of the Holy Spirit is for a Body to rise up that will truly partner with Him to stand in the gap between what is here and what is to come. We are calling for something apostolic to rise up, and it is necessary during this phase that we do not make claims prematurely. What is coming is greater than what is here; when that arrives, we will need to decrease. Indeed, for John this eventually meant he lost his head, and I suggest that there will be some current heads that will need to be removed when a new apostolic dimension rises.

If Malachi 4:6, which speaks of the hearts of parents and children being reconciled, has helped shape us over these past few years, I suggest that we will now have to embrace Jesus' words that *"Freely you have received, freely give"* (Matthew 10:8). Even if we have paid a price for something, the grace of Jesus means that we have received it freely. If we received it freely, we are not owners of it but stewards. If we are stewards we need to be wise, but if we are not owners, we have to give it away freely.

The idea that one generation received something through paying a price and any subsequent generation will have to go the same route is false. Whatever we have received is for the benefit of those who are coming. Our ceiling needs to become the floor for the next generation. They can then build in ways that we were not able to.

I believe this is a time for fulfillments, a time for investing into the rising generation. It will soon be time to recognize that what we have longed for is becoming increasingly manifest; that will signal that we who have led must then give way. At that stage, if

God will further grace us, we can then partner with what is rising. It is possible to receive a fresh impartation but only as we reposition ourselves.

It is a time for partnership, and earlier in this chapter I mentioned that before I ended this chapter I would touch on a perspective concerning why I regard North America as also being European. I do this now as I want to put a marker down that, just as the UK must embrace Europe, so Europe and North America must embrace each other.

North America and Europe

I will limit my comments to the North American continent, although it might also be possible to make the case that many other parts of the world can equally be described as "European," particularly due to the strong influence of the Greek and Roman empires (and Athens in particular) on modern culture.

In 2000 I had a dream and in this dream I saw a map of Northern America. The map was old, so I knew that it had some implication for understanding history. Two aspects surprised me: first, there was no Canadian/US border. However, given that it was an older map, that aspect should not have been too much of a surprise. It was the second aspect that held the real surprise for me. Across the continent were written the names of different European nations. In some ways the map looked like ones that can be purchased where the original native tribal names are written across the land, only the one in my dream had no tribal names – only the names of European nations.

The history of North America is the history of European conquest and abuse. There is no question that there are major areas of reconciliation that need to be worked through with respect to the native Americans, but the history means that the problems are not simply North American problems, but European ones.[1] Repentance is our responsibility as it was our forefathers who committed the sins. The enemy would love to keep the church in the UK and the US apart through cynicism on our part. However, we have to embrace our brothers and, as we find repentance together, this will take us out into other areas of our world.

In August 2001 I was participating in a conference with Lou Engle (the visionary behind the prayer gatherings known as "The Call") and in the context of prophesying into northern California I found myself saying:

> "There is a calling from Europe, there is a calling for the sons and daughters of North America to come and to bring help, there is a calling, there is a calling, for I declare, North America, that this is your time to come and begin to help in Europe. There is a calling in Europe, there is a calling in Europe, because there is a calling in the Middle East. There is a calling in the Middle East, but for that call to be responded to, there must be a response in North America, there must be a twinning of North America with Europe in order that the Middle East can be impacted, in order that the glory of God can once again flow."

The Lord is calling the church to revival, to be awakened, so that a day of true fulfillments can be our experience. This call will also take the church to the Middle East. Could it be that the glory of God will spread back to the trouble spots of our world? This is our time to respond as the fulfillment of God's promises are, in part, in the hands of the saints.

For this to take place we must not be sluggards but must make preparations for the visitation and habitation of God.

Note

1.   Richard Twiss's book *One Church Many Tribes* (Regal Books, 2000) is an excellent and enlightening read on the native American scene.

Chapter 2

Keys to the City

It was my good friend Jim Thwaites who first engaged me in conversation over the limited perspective I was carrying about reaching a city. At the time of the conversation I was promoting unity and prayer as the two key elements that needed to be in place for a city to be reached, and was passionately seeking to promote the former and provoke the latter. I certainly have not lessened my belief in the need of those two elements, but have gladly embraced the necessity of a third strand being brought alongside, that being the strand of releasing and empowering believers to be committed to and engaged with the diverse spheres of the city. Then, as mentioned in the Preface, I began to understand that we needed to separate out the prophetic watchperson role from that of the ongoing commitment to prayer across the city: thus acknowledging that there are four strands that are needed. (If the language sounds a little strange, please stick with it – I hope all will become clear.)

In the chapters that follow I will, with the help of Mike Love, seek to expand on these four aspects, while in this chapter I am simply introducing the concepts. Although there might be other ways of describing these ingredients, I suggest the four elements of prayer, prophetic watch ministry, leadership, and engaging with the spheres are foundational and need to be developed and established.[1] I do not want to convey the idea that God will not move till these four aspects are in place, as if He is subject to our activity; nor do I wish to suggest that reaching our region is simply a question of implementing the right strategy. However, I believe that we need to be as responsible as we can in applying ourselves to the release of these elements in our city or region.

The remainder of this chapter will simply outline the four aspects and sketch how they can be developed. The chapters that follow will then place a lot more meat on the bones.

Leadership

Leadership is a gift from God and many of us have had the bad experience of being in a situation where there has been a lack of clear leadership. In the same way that this is true within a local setting, so it is true in the setting of a city. A lack of city-wide leadership can be so debilitating to progress. Conversely, many of us also have had the bad experience of over-controlling leadership where no one is released and the only vision that counts is that of the person or people with official leadership titles.

Both experiences often stem from fear within those in leadership. Fear of making mistakes or of what people will say can paralyze leaders from setting out a direction, and fear of losing control or becoming redundant often results in leaders who hold on to control.

So much of this is resolved when we abandon the concept of leadership as being "leadership over" to the concept of leadership being "leadership within" (a church or a city). Jesus Himself said that His followers were not to lord it *over* and that He was one who was *among* them to serve (Luke 22:25–27). All bodies need leadership, but we certainly do not need dictatorship.

A process has been underway now for some time. The shorthand phrase "pastoring the city" has become a useful handle to keep us focused on one of our main goals, namely that of reaching the city as a whole. It has been great to have those who have pastored churches confess that their church is only one congregation of the whole Body in a region. It has been wonderful to see them embrace one another and together take on responsibility for the whole geography where they and their colleagues are situated. Leadership unity is, indeed, precious.

If only more cities could experience this, we would be a long way further down the road than we are. However, effectively pastoring the city is not going to be achieved by simply having all the church pastors together, but by releasing those people who will take responsibility for all the different areas of the city. These are the ones who together are called to stand in a pastoral role for the city as a whole. In other words, we cannot draw a straight line from "pastors recognizing they are pastoring a congregation of the one church" to "pastors who once pastored congregations now together pastoring the city as a whole." If that was the progress we saw take place, we would likely discover that the church was being pastored but the city remained uncared for.

The line that we draw from "church pastoring" to "city pastoring" is not straight, and there is at least one very definite and wonderful detour. There are many spiritual leaders for our regions who do not have time to easily conform to our church schedules, and I believe the Holy Spirit is pleased that they don't have this time. Their commitments lie elsewhere and most of their time is spent outside the parameters of what we have called church. (We might even find that there are some potential city pastors who have become disjointed from church as it currently exists and are going to be released into city pastoring without coming back through the system that we have called "church.") Leaving on one side the issue just raised, and returning to the suggestion that many spiritually anointed leaders are already correctly positioned in the spheres that make up the city, we will soon discover that church leadership will have to learn to make a relational detour to support them (and be educated by them) in order that the pastoral people for the city rise up from within the many spheres of our cities. So a few paragraphs on these spheres will be in order, and then we might be able to plot some of the progress that is necessary.

Spheres of the city

Some of the key elements that have to be engaged and impacted within the city are: government, education, health, business and

the arts. Our desire is not to produce a Christianized place where
every aspect is sanctified through having a Bible verse on the top
of the letter heading, but where every sphere of the city is being
influenced to act in a godly way that genuinely enhances goodness and acts as a catalyst for the presence of God to come. As
believers work for the prosperity of their city (and by that I do
not simply mean economic prosperity), so it should draw out the
men and women of peace (see Jeremiah 29:7; Luke 10:1–12). Not
all of them will be Christians, but God will anoint them for their
task, and I believe a number will become God-fearers and some,
indeed, will become full believers in Christ.

If the appropriate people from the spheres are to be drawn
through to stand in their place in the city, it will be vital for a
number of the church leaders and ministries to take time to
come alongside them so that there can be a mutual influencing
one of the other. Those in the spheres will need to know how
their faith can make a difference – a difference that is beyond
where their faith simply makes ethical demands on them, or
where it requires them to witness. Ministries will need to learn of
the challenge that these people face so that they in turn can be
forced into finding ways of making their own teachings relevant
to life situations. Those church leaders will have much to learn,
but if God has anointed them to equip the saints, then those in
the spheres will also benefit enormously.

I suggest that this process of repositioning for some current
church leaders is exactly where a number of cities and regions
find themselves at this moment of time. The challenges are great
but the treasures to be released are beyond our wildest dreams.
The chapters of this book that follow will seek to track these
changes and tentatively suggest ways forward.

Prayer and prophetic watch ministry

Although it takes more than prayer to see a breakthrough,
without prayer there will be no birth and what is birthed will
not be sustained. Prayer brings about great changes, and I am
most grateful that God is a God who hears and answers prayer.

Many breakthroughs are going to come, not because we have prayed but because the prayers of previous generations are awaiting an answer in our time. Many prayer warriors have died but they have died in faith.

The challenge facing many leaders and also many who carry responsibility for different aspects of a city's life is to be dependent on prayer. By so stating it, I am not suggesting that prayer is meant to replace hard persistent work, but to acknowledge that without a prayer dimension we will never express our dependence on the Living God intervening. We need both prayer and disciplined hard work to be in place. It is through prayer that God can energize the hard work and also override all our corporate wisdom. Through prayer He can release a word that worldly wisdom would reject, but as we obey God a channel is opened for the Spirit of God to move.

In the coming chapters I will outline three broad types of prayer. These are: ongoing, strategic and prophetic prayer. All three types are, I believe, necessary, although I do not believe that everyone will necessarily be able to embrace all three. This is not a problem, as our unity is not based on everyone agreeing on every point. There is a deeper unity that we have to contend for and this will mean, in the context of prayer, that we will gladly grapple with how we can effectively see people released in these different ways. We will have to work our way through this relationally as inevitably (and rightly so) there are different beliefs on such thorny issues as spiritual warfare.

Unity does not mean that we all believe the same thing. In fact, I am not too sure that God is committed to bring us to that type of unity. He is committed to us working together, though, because we love one another and believe the best about one another.

If we wish to see prayer developed through to the place where a city is being spiritually "harnessed," that prayer will include the basic ongoing daily prayers of the saints. That, indeed, is perhaps the most important element in prayer for it provides the foundation for everything else. In theory all believers should be able to buy into this type of praying, and nothing must be done to discourage that. However, I also suggest that there is a very real place in the city for the development of strategic prayer that increasingly covers every aspect of the life of the city. Finally, I believe there is the need for prophetic prayer and the release of those who have been gifted by God for fulfilling a role that we can call being prophetic watchpeople. I am well aware that this type of ministry and the associated practices are controversial, but I suggest strongly that this is developed without demanding that everyone is in agreement. Unity is stronger than agreement, and we can hold together even when there is disagreement. That is the heart of the gospel for it is through the gospel that former divides are healed.

In the chart on page 35 I plot what needs to take place. The descriptions are a guide rather than an accurate map. There is a critical phase of those in current (church) leadership being willing to move relationally to stand alongside those in the spheres – and it needs to be emphasized that it is "alongside" not "above." This has to coincide with a calling from those within the spheres for this, and from that meeting point we will begin to see emerge those who are called of God to "pastor the city." Prayer will fuel this whole process. Thus, I am suggesting that these four elements need to be in place for effective city-reaching to move forward. (Where there are different descriptions under the headings of "Leadership" and "Spheres" in the chart there is a suggested development that takes place from left to right. The key part is where there is a profitable inter-relationship between these two: indicated by the two-way arrow.)

If we were to express what is being proposed in diagram form, this would consist of four overlapping circles, with the pastoring of the city resulting from the interaction of those four over-lapping circles. The goal is not to impose a new structure, but to create a canopy over a city, and an involvement with a city, so that a harvest of righteousness rises up.

1. Leadership

In competition/my church must grow	Unity events/ friendship	One congregation of city church	A seeing of the spheres; being willing to be drawn out relationally; sitting alongside to learn	The city being pastored: some of the current pastors will also be city pastors – some will not; however some from the spheres and from the army of intercessors will also be city pastors

2. Spheres: e.g. arts; health; education; government; business

Not called, only "full-time ministries" are called	Have a purpose – but normally only understood as raising finance for church projects	Called to see godliness expressed in the sphere; and to draw the good out of the sphere	A drawing on ministry gifts for equipping	

3. All kinds of prayer

Ongoing that deepens and broadens. Saints praying, churches praying

Strategic that begins to cover the geographical and demographical aspects of the city, the key institutions and the points of entry to the community

4. Prophetic watch ministry

These people called to hear God for heaven's agenda and so to fuel the ongoing praying that takes place. Their anointing will bring a focus to the strategic level prayer. The end desire is the removal of blockages caused through past pollution and release the destiny of the city

Note

1. We also need to emphasize that the context for ministry in the city has to carry a genuine element of ministry among and to those who are marginalized. The advance of God's kingdom always carries justice at its heart. This emphasis might be served by making it another distinct element, so that it is not minimized. At the very least it has to flow through all the other four elements we are describing.

Chapter 3

Church in the City

"Failure is the foundation of truth. It teaches us what isn't true, and that is a great beginning. To fear failure is to fear the possibility of truth."   (Joan Chittister)

Much of what follows arises from working these things out on the ground in the city of Leeds where I have had the privilege of partnership in the gospel with many wonderful and inspiring people for whom Leeds is home, but also with some who have freely and sacrificially given to a city that is not their home. Foremost amongst this latter group, and the inspiration for many others to do likewise, is Martin Scott. He has given at least two weeks a year since 1998 to bring teams to pray with us and prophesy a hope and a future for our city, and to give a rich and deep theological understanding of what it takes to begin to see a city turn.

If Martin is right about the typology of the seven cities in Revelation with Ephesus as a "first city" (see Chapter 9), and if he is right that Leeds is a "first city," then a lot of trial and error is par for the course. It means that, for a city like Leeds, the prophetic is vital for the church to be effective; it also means that the church is itself prophetic in what it does. As with every kind of prophetic manifestation this has to be weighed by others. There are some good news stories to tell about what has happened in Leeds, some lessons we have learned that may be helpful elsewhere, and some new thinking, not yet fully formed, about what it means to be the church in the city, of the city, and for the city. Obviously the story I tell about Leeds is from my perspective only and I make no claim to the official version! Leeds has a lower than average church-going population; subjectively we are much more aware of weakness than strength, but we have come to believe that the weakness of the church in Leeds is her strength.

In these chapters I am going to look at how a radical approach to unity changes the way we do church, and how a radical redefinition of church changes the way we understand ministry.

From disunity to a unity

I want to take some time to describe the unity journey because I think it is important, and is a reminder not to forget the way we have traveled.

Disunity

Few people would disagree that the disunity of the Christian church is a scandal. We proclaim that God is three persons in one and that we, who were alienated from Him, and from one another, have been reconciled by His costly love. Our failure to live out who God is and what He has done has been almost fatal to the effectiveness of the gospel. There are many Christians who have given up on church because of their experiences of disunity; how many more people are there who, surveys suggest, rate Jesus, and even call themselves Christians, but do not want to know about the church? We have not been silent about unity, but we have spoken of it in a congregational or denominational setting, whilst being content to let disunity remain outside our own walls.

Disunity brings with it powerlessness against evil powers, broken-down walls and cities laid waste. Jesus said, *"Every kingdom divided against itself is laid waste; and no city or house divided against itself will stand"* (Matthew 12:25 NRSV). We devalue unity at our peril! This was graphically illustrated for me in the late 1980s during a prayer lunch for church leaders at which we had a Chinese church planter visiting us. When invited to comment, she said that as we prayed she had "seen" a celebration in the heavens over the city, but that it was a demonic celebration! She asked the Lord what could shift this and heard the answer, "The unity of My church."

One of my favorite definitions of revival is "a community saturated with the presence of God." In Ephesians 2:22, Paul says if we are not being built together, then there is no place for God to dwell. We know from Revelation that God fully intends to make His dwelling among us. Are our cities marked by God's presence, or by His absence?

Ecumenism

The ecumenical movement has addressed this disunity at a structural level with churches together groups and denominational dialogue. This has been viewed with mistrust by many evangelicals who have accused it of watering down the gospel into a lowest common denominator of social and political action. From the standpoint of the ecumenical movement it appears that evangelicals want nothing to do with the rest of the church. In Leeds the ecumenical process historically has struggled due to lack of commitment and energy.

Unity in the Spirit

A different kind of unity arose in the Charismatic Renewal in the 1960s and 1970s. Whereas Pentecostalism had its roots in remarkable racial reconciliation in Los Angeles but developed into a separatist movement, there was hardly a denomination unaffected by the Charismatic Renewal. Unity in the Spirit was not dependent on structural ecumenism. New worship music crossed denominational boundaries and there was a shared exploration of community and of spiritual gifts. Having been taken to a Pentecostal church when I was converted in 1976, my first experience of Charismatics two years later (which felt a bit risky!) at David Watson's Whole Story mission in Leeds came as a breath of fresh air, with its rather more contemporary approach. Following on from the Whole Story a group of evangelical and Charismatic leaders came together to explore what might happen next. Despite a strong leading to pursue relational unity rather than work on another project, it was decided to do another mission.

David Watson was instrumental in opening many doors into UK churches for John Wimber in the mid 1980s and with him a fresh wave of the Spirit focused more on evangelism and healing. Wimber also carried a burden for unity and hearing him speak of God's love for the whole church had an enormous impact on me.

In the late 1980s Charismatics Gerald Coates, Graham Kendrick, Roger Forster and Lynn Green launched March for Jesus which, during the next decade, saw hundreds of thousands of Christians world-wide out on the streets of their towns and cities in united praise, prayer and witness. Leeds had its first March for Jesus in 1989 and 5,000 people from Leeds and the region joined in. The networking that enabled March for Jesus to happen seemed too important to drop but, although we had a couple of regional gatherings of leaders from the Charismatic end of the spectrum, we did not know how to proceed. In Leeds, inspired by the Prayer for Revival meetings in Birmingham, we started monthly prayer for revival meetings sponsored by four or five churches in the city, and we sensed God's presence and pleasure as we prayed for the city.

Following on from March for Jesus came Challenge 2000, the English version of DAWN 2000. National church census figures formed the backdrop for denominational and stream leaders to set national goals for church planting to be fulfilled by 2000. For the first time, church leaders were being encouraged to look together at the city strategically, and then plant churches in the least churched areas, or at the very least adhere to a church planting protocol in an attempt to avoid some of the hurt and misunderstanding caused by new church plants in the 1970s and 1980s. The story in Numbers 32 seemed to leap off the page and demand that we stop concerning ourselves exclusively with our own church and ministry and take on the task of helping each other in the taking of territory. And the story of Nehemiah provided a rationale for both reaching a whole town or city and for each church working locally to do so. It placed our local working into the bigger context of seeing the wall of the city rebuilt and the city restored. The Building Together network that both Martin and I are involved with, had its beginnings in this season to help equip churches to be catalysts towards fulfilling these goals.

Through Ed Silvoso we started to hear of the revival in Argentina where it seemed unity between leaders in cities was the prerequisite for effective prayer to pull down city-based strongholds and bring about an atmosphere conducive to evangelism. Fueled by hunger for revival, with a focus on city reaching, we saw that unity and prayer were the starting points. In the early 1990s the people giving themselves to these strategies were few and far between and Building Together was a vital gathering for encouragement and inspiration. In 1994 the Holy Spirit fell on us powerfully as we met in London and we have been committed to follow His leading since then.

By the late 1990s in Leeds the strategy had run out of steam, leaving us with a small monthly prayer breakfast for leaders and a monthly City Watch prayer meeting. But then in 1998 we had two weeks of Sowing Seeds for Revival with Martin and a team of people from other parts of the country. Through that fortnight we began to hear what the Spirit was saying to the church in Leeds. There were not many of us, and there was nothing special about those who were there, but God was there. Since then we have spent twelve weeks doing the same thing, as well as two weeks in Lille, our twin city in northern France, and several hundred people have joined in from many different churches. I cannot overstate the importance for us of this prophetic input. It has exposed and pulled down strongholds in our thinking, sown seeds of hope and faith, given us insight into the nature and personality of the city, and given us strategy to pursue. In addition to the Sowing Seeds for Revival weeks we have had many other people come on prayer teams to hold up our arms in prayer and to keep believing when we doubted. The story of how God has led us and spoken to us would take too much more space here but some of it is on *Network: Leeds*, a new communication strategy that is in its pilot stage.[1]

By the end of the 1990s the national picture was very different from the beginning of the decade with barely a town of any size without some expression of united leadership and prayer at the evangelical/Charismatic end of the church spectrum.

Another significant change had happened by the close of the millennium. The church leaders of longest standing in many communities were now the "new church" Charismatics. Denominational ministers move on within their denominations but there really isn't anywhere for non-denominational leaders to go. By default they had become the elders. The distribution of Sentinel's *Transformation* videos broke all predictions and connected a whole new constituency with a vision, not just for revival and church growth, but for real social transformation. God used the stories to lift the eyes of many from a focus on building church to a vision of a city transformed. Some who argue that building the church is the proper task of ministry and that the message of *Transformations* is a distraction need to be reminded that it is Jesus who builds His church and it is for us to seek the Kingdom, which is "God's transforming action in the world!"[2]

Unity from humility

In Leeds we have seen these two journeys, the ecumenical and the Charismatic, begin to coincide. We Charismatics have found many wonderful people committed to unity and social transformation in the ecumenical movement, which can itself be energized in partnership with the evangelical churches and renewed by the expression of the Spirit at work in Pentecostals and Charismatics. Many evangelicals are engaging with the spiritualities of the historic denominations, and with denominational loyalties weakening it seems that God is bringing His people together.

God usually looks for humility and often brokenness before He gets to work. Despite all our prayers and faith for church growth, church planting and revival, at the end of the 1990s, the Decade of Evangelism, we had seen decline in church attendance in England. In fact, we now know that this decline, bad enough in the 1980s, accelerated sharply during the 1990s. Michael Moynagh's analysis of the trend suggests fewer than 1 per cent of the population will be in church on an average Sunday in thirteen years' time, a decline of over 90 per cent from the beginning of the Decade of Evangelism![3] Some denominations are now facing extinction, and the heady optimism of the new churches during the 1980s and early 1990s has been tempered by stagnation in growth and spiritual life. In this context there is a surprising openness and humility amongst leaders of the historic churches to radical thinking about the state of the church that is sometimes lacking in leaders of the new churches.

A former professor of theology at Leeds recently warned the non-evangelical churches engaged in outworking a social gospel that without a personal gospel there will be no church to engage with the injustices of the city! On the other hand, an increasing number of younger evangelicals and Charismatics are engaging with issues of trade and social justice, and finding a purely personal and church-based spirituality to be unsatisfying and barren. The goal of church growth suddenly seems to be past its sell-by date as the potential for the people of God to effect real change dawns on us. With humility we evangelicals are recognizing how far we have fallen from the standards set by the great evangelical social reformers of the eighteenth and nineteenth centuries, and we see that we have a lot to learn from those Christians who have been involved in these issues, for "the church is not an end in itself. The growth and prosperity of the church is not the goal of history."[4]

And lastly, perhaps God, having heard our prayers and seen our faith, now wants to pour out the new wine of the Kingdom but has had to wait for us to be willing to let go of an old wineskin. Perhaps God in His mercy has had to judge His household: haven't our denominational and congregational loyalties hidden a multitude of sins – pride, jealousy, unforgiveness, and self-ishness? Is there really any difference between the church in Corinth and the church in my city, so long as we keep aloof from one another and enshrine our distinctives (what makes us better than other congregations/streams/denominations) and our vision (why you should follow me/us rather than anyone else) in our church publicity? Could Paul's critique of the Corinthian church be equally true for us, evidenced by a lack of the power and the presence of God in our cities? Once again the church must become a missionary church and "everything about ... a missionary situation conspires to make Christian disunity an intolerable anomaly. Within the assumed unity of Christendom, the Churches could fall apart, increasingly leaving the main direction of the life of the world to secular forces, and concentrating on rival interpretations of the life in Christ ... When the church faces outwards towards the world it knows that it only exists as the first-fruits and the instrument of that reconciling work of Christ, and that division within its own life is a violent contradiction of its own fundamental nature."[5]

Opportunity
Not only is it a time of crisis for the church but also a time of great opportunity. The American Christian activist Jim Wallis,[6] after a recent meeting with the UK Cabinet, reported that the UK church now had the kind of opportunities for which he had prayed in the US for many years, but never thought he would see. The Chancellor Gordon Brown in discussion with Steve Chalke asked how the church could be roused from its retirement to take its place in public life. Locally there are more opportunities for Christians to be involved in decision-making bodies that have real power to effect change, than there are Christians willing to take them. Government is concerned about the decline in social capital – people who freely give of their time and resources to other people and groups in society – and knows that it is still Christians who provide a disproportionate amount of that social capital. If social capital is on the wane, spiritual capital certainly isn't. The 2001 National Census results show that 70 per cent of people still choose to describe themselves as Christian, despite having the option of saying they have no religion or of not disclosing their religion. Spirituality, having been pushed to the margins of irrelevancy and superstition by modernity, is back with a vengeance in post-modernity. The

increasing distrust of politics and politicians is giving rise to direct action and community involvement. People who never before publicly protested went onto the streets to challenge the British and American governments' decision to invade Iraq – and for once church leaders spoke with one voice and found common cause with the people.

The present opportunities, and challenges, for the church's mission demand that we bury our differences and begin to recognize and combine the remarkable resources of the Body of Christ.

What kind of unity?

An important shift in my thinking about unity came a few years ago when I realized that the Body of Christ *is* a unity. Until that time I had believed that unity was a matter of getting church leaders together, physically and mentally, and then getting congregations together for worship, prayer, and ... well, for what? I believed that we would have to have achieved a considerable degree of such unity before we could see the kind of things Ed Silvoso, for example, talked about. Unity worthy of the name must be unity across difference: it is reconciliation of irreconcilables. But the starting point for this kind of unity (in our thinking) is the "local church," inviolable and fixed for all time. I still believe these things are important but this central focus on the local church is one of the "immaculate assumptions"[7] we make when we think about church that tramlines our thinking. The reality is somewhat different.

The Body of Christ *is one*, and all who are in Christ by grace though faith are part of it. From Him, the head, the whole body is joined together in all its diversity. We cannot create unity, we can destroy it, but we should *"make every effort to keep"* it (Ephesians 4:3). If we say the church is the Body of Christ, we start with our assumptions about local church and then we try to think of this body within a congregational shape. But if we say the Body of Christ is the church, we set our thinking and our practice free.[8] All who are in Christ are part of His body and He is the head. There is an organic and invisible unity of all God's people who have one Father, one Head and are joined with one another and with God by the Spirit. As Paul says,

> *"Now you are the body of Christ, and each one of you is a part of it."* (1 Corinthians 12:27)

There is still the tension between the individual and the corporate, but the corporate in view here is not the congregation we belong to, but the Body of Christ we are part of. The structures that have profile on the landscape of the city – local churches, denominational structures, para-church organizations – hinder, rather than help, us from seeing this truth. These expressions of church have had the monopoly on what constitutes a valid church and have arrogated to themselves the name "church." They have done so in the face of one of our earliest creedal affirmations: there is one holy, catholic and apostolic church.

Networks

What kind of structure would help us to discern the Body of Christ in the city better? There is a rapidly growing understanding and body of literature about networks. I opened a magazine this morning and the first two pages were a double-page advertisement for a computer company extolling the awesome power of the network. Business is increasingly being done through networks. Social movements have the ability to mobilize large numbers of people and effect change in society and do so by networking. The Internet gives us a model of how networks form and what can flow through them.[9] The human body is a network of blood vessels and nerves that enable it to function. Could it be that the network is a truer expression of the Body of Christ than the congregation-centered structures that are based on out-moded organizational structures? Thinking of the Body of Christ as a complex network of individuals bound together by the Spirit, apparently anarchic but actually under the headship of Christ, gives us a very different kind of unity. This unity is relational, complex and organic, arising from and embedded in the contexts in which we find ourselves in the city. It takes seriously the inalienable truth that the Body of Christ is a unity. It could be the flexible wineskin we need in a post-modern world.

The first kind of unity, the unity of church leaders and congregations, is the necessary precursor for the second kind of unity. The people of God will be permissioned and affirmed to take part in the network by their congregational leaders because there is a culture of trust and working together amongst them. People are obviously free to join in anyway but it would be better to do so with blessing. It could be that as the network waxes the congregation wanes, and congregation leaders have to consider the cost of continuing to release people to the network. But this points to an important truth: unity kills! Taking unity seriously exposes and then puts to death the kind of sins, referred to above, inherent in the way we have done church. We will need to question whether it even matters if our congregations continue to exist as separate entities.

A fruit-bearing vine

The metaphor of the vine in John 15 further defines the network. The network derives from, and is vitally linked to, Jesus Himself who lives in it and expresses Himself through it. To the extent that this is true, the network bears fruit as prayer is heard. Where there is unity God commands blessing, and the blessing is life (Psalm 133:3). Unity without fruit is a barren unity, and God's intent is that children are born within covenantal relationship. These kinds of relationships are fruitful because they are the conduits for the Spirit of God, and our experience in Leeds has been that these kinds of relationships do bear fruit. There are now a number of city-wide initiatives that have grown out of a commonly perceived need or opportunity and have become a reality because of this kind of unity – *"being like-minded ... being one in spirit and purpose"* (Philippians 2:2). They are not para-church and they are not local church, but are expressions of the church in Leeds.[10]

Typically at leadership level they involve leaders of different congregations and others, and the people involved also come from different congregations. In some cases people who come to faith through these projects may not find their way into the congregations that originally sponsored them, but that does not seem to matter as long as they are connected in to the Body of Christ in a way that is conducive to their growth. This is likely to be the case particularly amongst young people. We may well see new expressions of church being birthed that will pull existing models of church into new shapes, and existing church leaders into new responsibilities.

Geography and unity

To conclude and complete this chapter on unity, we need to take a look at unity and geography. The two defining criteria for our unity are Christ and the city. Paul saw the church in Colossians 1:2 as *"the saints and faithful brothers and sisters in Christ at Colossae"* (NRSV). As we have already seen, the church is one by virtue of being *"in Christ" and* we are one with all who are in Christ in Leeds. It is for us to live up to this calling (Ephesians 4:1–16). Our geographic location is not random; it is God who has planted us – we, the children of the Kingdom, are strategically sown in the field of the world by the Son of Man (Matthew 13:38). In Revelation 2 and 3 the Lord speaks to the churches in the seven cities of Asia Minor whose identity, destiny and character are so clearly bound up with the cities they each inhabit. The church shapes the city, or the city shapes the church, and woe to the churches that think they are above such things. The transformation of the city of Leeds is the task assigned to the church in Leeds in each generation. Jesus taught that the reward of the faithful servants is the stewardship of cities (Luke 19:17–19).

> "To make cities – that is what we are here for. To make good cities – that is for the present hour the main work of Christianity. For the city is strategic ... Whoever makes the city makes the world ... When Christianity shall take upon itself in full responsibility the burden and care of cities the Kingdom of God will openly come on earth. What

Christianity waits for also, as its final apologetic and justifi-
cation to the world, is the founding of a city which shall be
in visible reality a city of God."[11]

Relationships we have enjoyed and benefited from in our
streams and denominations have been about identity. We have
been, or become, part of groupings with like-minded people and
have spent time getting to know one another at a national or
even international level, praying together, worshiping together,
learning together, and undoubtedly been helped in our local
churches. However, if we are to take seriously our mission calling
and mandate in our own city, we will certainly need to give
priority, or at least equality, to relationships locally and inevitably they will be relationships with people and churches that
are not like us!

Abraham was able to intercede for the town of Sodom because
he was privy to God's plans and so entered into intercession for
the city to be spared. As we, the church in our own town, seek
God together, surely God is no less likely to let us in on His plans
for our town. In my own city there has been little strategic
engagement at church leader level about the city as a whole.
Most denominational leaders oversee regions that are wider than
Leeds and are thus not mandated to focus on this particular
city. New church stream leaders are likely to have an even larger
territory to oversee and may have little or no knowledge of
Leeds. So we have regional or national leadership concentrating
on an area larger than Leeds, and local church leadership
focusing on their part of the city, with little or nothing in-
between. There is no mechanism for the church to engage with
those bodies and powers that are concerned with the city as a
whole. A city is a solidarity with its particular dimensions of
principalities and powers, and it is only the solidarity of the city
church that is able to take on the city and its powers effectively
and see them bow to the Lordship of Jesus. In those cities and
towns where this problem has been addressed and there is
effective engagement of the church at town or citywide level,
there has been a marked increase of Kingdom influence.

When we engage with any part of the city, we also engage with the city principalities and powers, the spiritual history of the city, as well as the word and calling of God to the city. In other words it is not enough just to engage locally. In our immediate area there are two mosques – one a former Roman Catholic parish church, the other an imposing brand new building – and a Hindu temple. And just along the street from our church building is the Sorcerer's Apprentice, once the largest mail order supplier of occult materials in Europe. We realized a long time ago that we were unable to take on the principalities and powers alone. We have learned from Nehemiah the futility of only building up our section of the wall without reference to how the rest of the wall is to be built.

Furthermore, there is no strategic channeling of resources to the neediest areas of the city where the churches are likely to be weaker and less able to cope with the demands of inner-city mission and ministry. This results in new church plants being concentrated in the already most churched area of the city, and little understanding of the Body of Christ in the city looking after its weaker members.

Summary

The Spirit of God has been at work in the ecumenical movement and in the Charismatic/evangelical churches and there has been an increase of unity in many towns and cities. During the 1990s there was an increase of united prayer for cities and a growing awareness of the mission of the church to reach cities and see city transformation. Churches across the board have been humbled by decline or stagnation but this humility has enabled them to see that we face common challenges in an increasingly post-Christendom society, and yet also great opportunities to re-engage with post-modern people and society. But unity is more radical than simply doing what we have done but now doing it together. In all the discussion about the nature of church we could start to see church as the people of God awesomely networked together in the Spirit under the headship of Christ.

Human leadership and structures are relativized in this paradigm of church. Networked unity is relational unity, and we can expect to see fruit in the birth of new expressions of church. These will pull the church into new shapes and new understandings of leadership. The context in which all this is worked out is the mission field of the territory God has called us to at the time and we engage with it strategically on earth and in the heavens. And all this means that a new kind of church leadership is urgently needed.

Notes

1. www.networkleeds.com
2. G.R. Beasley-Murray, *Jesus and the Kingdom of God* (Eerdmans, 1986).
3. Michael Moynagh, *Changing World, Changing Church* (Monarch, 2001), p. 12.
4. Lesslie Newbigin, *The Gospel in a Pluralist Society* (Eerdmans, 1989), pp. 133–4.
5. Lesslie Newbigin, *The Household of God* (Paternoster, 1998).
6. *SojoMail*, 4 June 2001.
7. Tom Sine, *Mustard Seed versus McWorld* (Monarch, 1999).
8. Pete Ward, *Liquid Church* (Hendrickson and Paternoster, 2002), p. 37.
9. Manuel Castells, *The Rise of the Networked Society* (Blackwell, 1996).
10. Some examples are: Leeds Faith in Schools – a team of schools workers; Kidz Klub – a city-wide children's church for unchurched children; Youth Cell Network – peer-led cell groups made up of young people from one or more congregations or none or based in schools; Transform – a year-long training program based in Leeds and Bradford; Leeds Asian Ministries – outreach to Asian minorities and refugees; Leeds Asylum Seeker Network + Welcome to Leeds – outreach to asylum seekers and refugees; an informal team of people giving support to University CUs.
11. Henry Drummond, *The City without a Church* (Hodder & Stoughton, 1988), p. 12.

Chapter 4

Leadership in the City Church

All of these developments call for a new kind of leadership to emerge as well as new understandings of God's purpose for entire cities and for new models of church. Existing leadership at local church or denominational level is inadequate for true ecumenism – the whole church embracing the whole city. What is also clear is that existing models of church leadership are not transferable to a city-wide context, if we are to be church in the city in more than name alone. Whilst we may be happy to have a clear leadership structure for our own congregation, denomination and stream, many would rightly resist the same kind of leadership at city level. Sociologically most, if not all, organizations are pyramid shaped. Visionary leadership is at the apex of the pyramid and the resources of the organization are harnessed to serve that vision. So we are likely to ask about the vision and leadership of an organization before we join ourselves to it and put our energies into it. This is true at local church level and churches looking to align themselves to a denomination or stream will ask similar questions. We might term these kinds of relationships vertical relationships in that they fit into a hierarchy of authority, however loose. These kinds of relationships are about our identity, where we fit, our kind of people. Relationships across the city are different. They will have to be with people different from us, with whom the fit is not as easy. The establishment of another tier of hierarchy at city level to which churches submit would be as impossible as it would be unpalatable. While there are some cities around the world where the leader of the largest church is thereby likely to be the leader of a city-wide grouping, it is unlikely that this grouping will be able to encompass anything like the breadth of the Body of Christ. George Otis notes that there are no mega-churches in the communities where he has identified true transformation taking place. It is almost as if the presence of a mega-church will hinder the emergence of a different kind of leadership at city level. This is largely due to the self-sufficiency of the mega-church and the mega-gifting of the mega-church leader. The crunch issue is: are we primarily committed to building our own church or are we primarily committed to seeking the increase of the Kingdom of God in our town or city? In theory these two priorities are not necessarily mutually exclusive, but in practice they often are.

What is needed, then, are relationships for the sake of territory. These will need to take priority over the relationships we have for the sake of identity, if we are to take seriously the task of reaching the territory. If relationships in a vertical authority structure are not the way to work together in the city, we need to discover a way of relating in a horizontal or flat structure. Whereas previously our structures determined our relationships, now our relationships must determine our structures – and our relationships must be local, though obviously not exclusively so. From a denominational perspective we may know people at the other end of the country a lot better than our fellow laborers in our own town or city. If we recognize that we are truly the Body of Christ with all of God's people in our city, and then invest the same priority and value into these local relationships as we have done into our denominational structures, we will avoid the sin of the two tribes in Numbers 32 and see the Body of Christ built up to reach the whole city effectively.

We may agree that a hierarchical city leadership would be unpalatable and give up on the idea because we cannot conceive of any other way of doing it. However, there are models being developed that recognize the need for visionaries but avoid the hierarchical pyramid. In an equality of interaction with others vision for the city grows as different giftings and insights are brought to bear on the process of seeking God's vision and its outworking. This vision is central and grips our hearts and imaginations; we could also say that Jesus becomes central. Leadership is amongst, rather than over, other church leaders and may move from one to the other under the dancing hand of the Spirit. Think of Joshua preparing to take his first city – his encounter with the Lord gets his perspective right. It is not whether the Lord is on our side but whether we are on His, because if we are going to take cities He must take command. And His command relativizes all human command! If church leaders can begin to work like this, it will be good news for the city and bad news for the enemies of God! The vision for our city, and indeed our knowledge of Jesus, grows and becomes richer as others contribute their insights in a multi-voiced equality. New values emerge in this way of working together as brothers and sisters, and so a culture develops made up of new covenant values in the Holy Spirit. This culture is more powerful than the most powerful leader or well-run organization precisely because it is a new covenant culture able to get into people's hearts. Furthermore, this is an entrepreneurial culture where new leaders can emerge quickly.

Everybody a leader?

However, it is not just about changing the way that existing church leaders work, important though that is. There needs to be a radical reappraisal of our concepts of leadership in the church. A few years ago I asked a Ph.D. student doing a doctorate on decision-making in organizations to talk to me about our congregational structure. Her starting point was that vision comes bottom-up in organizations. She explained that values flow "top down" (or, more palatably, "inside out") and as people lay hold of values, their vision for how they and the organization might perform better flows bottom up, thus maximizing the potential locked up in people. I had learned that the task of Christian leadership was to cast vision and then obtain ownership of the vision in any and every way possible. I had been told that vision

+ vision = division. I had measured people's commitment by their commitment to the vision of the congregation, and judged success by how well we had achieved the vision. I realized the church had been serving my vision and that there was already a disintegration taking place with people in my congregation tiring of this vision-led approach.

Some weeks later I went to the second of the excellent Spring Harvest At Work Together conferences and heard more of what was to me a revolutionary way of understanding organizations. This bottom-up view calls for a change in understanding of leadership and management. Organizations are experimenting with "flat structures" rather than cumbersome hierarchies. An acquaintance I met there told me that the IT section of the large corporation he worked for was structured in this way. The IT world changes so fast that each operative in his section is empowered to take a lead as soon as an opportunity presents itself. The role of the manager (who is paid less than the people she manages) is to channel resources to the lead person. A hierarchical chain of command structure would respond too slowly and miss the opportunity. I found this lit up for me exciting new possibilities of how church could once again become a movement of ordinary people being Kingdom-active wherever they were in the city. I believe this to be one of the vital contributions of the G12 cell movement. A recent TV series on leadership began with the leadership style of Hitler. His rapid success in overrunning France in the early part of the Second World War was due to "operational command," the delegation of real strategic decision-making to field com-manders who knew what was happening before their own eyes better than central command. Hitler began to fail as he lost trust in his field commanders and assumed increasingly detailed command.

When vision of how a city might be transformed through the agency of the people of God comes into view, vision for the local church is relativised. We will see how this might work in a city context in the next chapter, but what are the implications for leadership of these two paradigm shifts?

Leadership across a city

Relationship

Let's start with the transition of present church leaders. The hierarchical model of leadership that operates in much of the church cannot transfer to leadership across a city, whether in church unity networks or in the networks of the people of God. Command and control will not work. Many effective church leaders might disqualify themselves at this point, finding it too difficult to work in a messy environment where it seems there is little or no power to effect change. Gifted and ambitious leaders may not be willing to "waste time" networking without apparent immediate purpose; but it is only long-term relationship-building which produces an environment of trust and respect that will produce lasting fruit. We know from John 15 that this is true for our relationship with the Lord, and our relationships with one another should be invested with the same values of "abiding" in unity. Tom Marshall suggests there are four basic elements to relationship: trust, love, respect, and understanding.[1] It is relationship that will enable us to step outside our "vertical" structures and appreciate differences rather than be threatened by them. It is in relationship that we learn that most important of graces, humility, as we genuinely consider others better than ourselves, admit our weaknesses and be glad of the strengths of others. To enter into relationship is to risk, and making new relationships may feel risky as we step outside our boundaries of safety. This kind of relational unity can be undermined by the mobility of Christian leaders, particularly in the denominational structures, but people are less likely to move from where they have strong relationships and people with a genuine vision for their town or city are more likely to stay put. These kinds of relationships are rare but urgently needed amongst Christian leaders. It seems that the very way we do church makes it difficult for leaders to have real relationships within the congregation, and we are often too busy for peer relationships with other leaders (and their spouses) in our area. This is good neither for them as people, nor for the mission of the church.

In Leeds, as in many towns, there have been retreats and consultations for leaders and a monthly prayer lunch, and we have tried to help build relationship through facilitating "eat and pray" triplets for leaders and spouses. We have encouraged evangelistic projects with churches working together, and have entered into a dialogue between African-Caribbean and white church leaders. Many of these things and more can be found in many towns and cities across the country.

Ed Silvoso uses the term "perimeters of unity," suggesting helpfully that we need to start where we are, with people with whom we have most in common as the first perimeter. We must not stop there, but we do not expect the same kind of unity the further out we go, as style and theology differ. Gathering for prayer or worship may foster unity within certain perimeters, but can hinder it outside those perimeters. Such a gathering is not devalued because it is not as wide as we might wish; Ed Silvoso argues that inclusivity should not be at the cost of cohesion. But we must not devalue unity with Christians with whom we might not be able to gather in these ways. Unity does not depend on what we can do in gatherings! As we develop friendship, we will find that the differences enrich us rather than threaten us.

Working together

In such an environment we can expect to see wider recognition and value given to the leadership and ministry gifts that God has given to the city church. These gifts can then come into full effectiveness in the building up of the Body of Christ in our towns and cities. The work of Christ in our cities and towns surely depends upon the Body of Christ coming to the full measure of Christ (Ephesians 4:1–16)! Congregation leaders praying together, humbly acknowledging their own weaknesses and the strengths of others without being threatened by them, recognizing they are called to the same mission field and their gifts are for the one church, having the same mind and committed to co-equipping the people of God in their strategic positioning in the mission field of the city – these things are more and more common. Then Tom, Dick and Harriet, working in one office but from three different congregations, can express the unity of the Body of Christ where it matters – before a watching world. They can agree in prayer and seek the Kingdom of God in their office and for their colleagues, and be fully endorsed and supported by their congregation leaders in doing so. Or on a larger scale church leaders working together, their gifts complementing one another, can resource a student Christian Union for mission and maturity without feeling the need to do their own student ministry on campus. Must we replicate our divisions amongst Christian students who have a unique opportunity at university to fellowship with believers from differing church backgrounds and to learn about, and benefit from, the unity of the Body of Christ?

In Leeds we have been able to start a city-wide Kidz Klub, with four churches initially partnering together to reach un-churched children with the love of God. A team of forty or more volunteers from up to fifteen churches visit over 1,000 children a week in their homes and up to 500 children are bussed in to a city-center church building for a Saturday morning of raucous music, crazy games and competitions, life lessons and learning about God. We are about to develop two area satellites in partnership with at least three local congregations for each satellite. There is also a city-wide network of peer-led youth cells supported and resourced by most of the Christian youth workers. Some cells are made up exclusively of young people from one congregation, but many have people from more than one or none. Starting with one inter-church cell four years ago there are now over twenty cells in the network. Leeds Faith in Schools, a team of schools workers led by Lee Jackson, was started as a Trust eight years ago but sees its context as the church in Leeds. Similar values underlie work with the South Asian community, asylum seekers and refugees, a Leeds and Bradford training program called Transform, work with the University CUs and large city-wide gatherings. In each case relational unity is the context in which these initiatives have their being, not as para-church organizations, but as new expressions of the church in Leeds. This is where much of the mission of the church is happening.

Initial questions about accountability from within a vertical
paradigm have largely faded away as a culture of greater horizontal accountability has been recognized. This culture counter-
acts kingdom building, personality cult and independence as it is
mutual and interdependent, and always has the mission field
of the city in view. Congregation leaders are not the leaders of
these initiatives but their support, endorsement and permission
have contributed enormously to an improved environment for
entrepreneurial mission.

Our experience of co-working in Leeds has been surprisingly
painless. It could be because we are focused around mission, or
because we are not trying to work out relationships in a
hierarchical model, but I suspect it has something to do with
the anointing that flows when God's children dwell in unity
(Psalm 133).

Christianarchy!

If congregation leaders are to take their place in leadership across
the city, they must not only be prepared to "waste" time on
relationship, they must also be prepared to work with apparent
anarchy amongst individuals, churches, denominational structures and Christian organizations that all have their own agenda.
Is this a field worth putting time and energy into? Why not
simply invest into building a church big enough to have
sufficient resources to go it alone and achieve more? But there
already is a mega-church like this in the city: the church of Jesus
Christ! To believe this takes faith! Just as chaos theory sees a deep
and mysterious order in apparent chaos, so there is a deep and
mysterious unity in the apparent anarchy of the Body of Christ.
He is the head, and this is no nominal, honorary title. Just as the
human body is a wonderful network of communication from the
head to the rest of the body and back again, so is the Body of
Christ by the Spirit. But just as a body can be severely handi-
capped by a breakdown in the nervous system, so too the Body of
Christ falls far short of the glory God has intended for it. Because
the unity of the Body of Christ exists, we can never create it, only

discover it. If we create groupings of unity, there is a real danger we do violence not only to the rest of the Body we exclude from our group, but also to the Head and to the Spirit. We can, however, bring healing to the Body through reconciliation and communication. We can seek to join up what has been broken apart. We can help to give the various parts of the Body the awareness that they are one with the rest. And we, like Jesus, can pray. Many years ago I had a picture of the church in Leeds as a man of great strength yet terribly deformed and twisted, walking slowly and painfully but nevertheless in the direction God wanted. As we begin to see connections made and the causes of division healed, we will see the Lord Jesus at work through His Body in remarkable and surprising ways, out of our control but in His. According to chaos theory each of us is only six handshakes away from George Bush, or anybody else on the planet. However, because we inhabit relatively closed relational groupings, the odds are much higher. All it takes to reduce these odds dramatically is for some individuals to be bridges between groupings. In other words, it is not necessary for every Christian to know every other Christian in the city for meaningful unity; all it takes is for some people to network the networks.

Five-fold ministry gifts

To serve this Body so that it comes to maturity, we will need the gifts Jesus has given for this purpose. There has been a renewed focus on the so-called five-fold ministry gifts in recent decades to correct the over-emphasis on the pastor–teacher ministry. In the UK we have seen the apostolic ministry understood mainly as the leader of a network or stream of new churches. We have understood that apostles, prophets and evangelists are primarily "trans-local" and therefore located them nationally or inter-nationally. Additionally we now need to locate them in our cities and towns. We may fight shy of doing this for all the reasons I have stated – fear of excessive authority and power in one person or group – but this is because we have associated these gifts with governmental authority rather than their equipping function.

Could it be that God has placed within His church in any given geography the gifts and ministries necessary for the fulfillment of His work there? At present, such ministry gifts operate almost exclusively within individual congregations, denominations or streams. What might happen if they were released to serve the whole Body for the sake of the work of God in the city? Can we imagine the following scenario where we live?

People with apostolic gifting being recognized, set apart and supported to break new ground in the unreached places and people groups of the city and to bring apostolic strategy to bear on the people of God, not just for the city, but from the city to other cities and nations.

Prophets coming together to hear what the Spirit is saying to the church (in line with the scriptural precedent that God does want to speak to His church in individual cities!) and equipping the people of God to be prophetic in every sphere of the life of the city – politics, business, education, justice, health, the arts and media, the poor. Evangelists strategizing together how to get the gospel to as many people as possible in as many ways as possible by as many people as possible, keeping the whole church to its evangelistic mandate of disciple making and providing resources and help for the task.

Teachers being set free from their largely ineffective weekly sermon making, to provide a learning environment for the people of God, equipping them with the tools to do theology where they are, recognizing and providing the many different levels of teaching needed by a maturing Body which is making disciples.

Pastors, in addition to caring for the flock, working together to see a full range of pastoral ministry come into place for the sick and wounded of our society – release from addictions, counseling ministries, therapeutic communities, family ministry, personal wholeness courses.

It may be an impossible dream but there are signs of hope that we are seeing something of the above come into being. Only the seriously large mega-church could hope to provide this range of ministry in one congregation, but God has intended it for His whole church. Some commentators on the present church scene see such mega-churches as an essential part of the future, able to provide the range of programs and services no smaller church could hope to provide. They will be the fittest who survive. There are huge problems with this analysis: the systematized and uniform approach of mega-churches will not accommodate a post-modern generation, and research shows beyond reasonable doubt that the bigger a church becomes, the less able it is to mobilize its members or to achieve, proportionately, the growth-by-conversion rates of smaller churches. Like out of town shopping malls that offer the consumer all they could possibly want and kill off local shops, the price for their success is the weakening and demise of the small and local expression of the church rooted in communities. Despite these inbuilt weaknesses, for some reason we still hold up big churches as successful models we should all try to emulate.

And elders

And finally, we need a new understanding of eldership. Different expressions of church have varying understandings of eldership operating at congregational level. As with so many of these things, we have read the New Testament through the lenses of a particular ecclesiology, which has the local congregation as its defining reference point. The Greek word *ekklesia* was used of a gathering of citizens which came together as a political body for city affairs, either lawfully and in order, or otherwise as in Ephesus. The very use of this word to describe the church suggests that it is now the church who have true governmental authority, who are the body politic of the coming Kingdom. I say "who," rather than "which," *because* history has shown that whenever the church as institution gains political power it is not edifying for anyone! If the church is the *ekklesia* of God in the city, then it is not unreasonable to look at elders in the same way. Elders were elders of the community at varying levels of responsibility – from family to city. They were not leaders; they were not priests or prophets. They ensured good order as they watched over the city and sat in the gate. They were the esteemed members of the community. It was perfectly reasonable for the early church community to appoint elders for the Christian community in any given place. As elders of the *ekklesia*, I suggest they were not only to bring order to the internal governance of the Christian community, but also to the role of the *ekklesia* as the body politic of the Kingdom of God in and for that city.

How can city eldership operate? Martin Scott helped us to see that identifying the elders is not constructive, but those people who are true elders will want to ensure that elders come into place! James Thwaites pointed out that the goal is not to have elders in place, but an "eldered culture" across the city. There is a danger in naming certain people as elders because, by default, people will look to them to be responsible, to take a lead. As we have seen, it is the saints who must take the lead, with the elders responsive to them rather than responsible for them. It is much more important to have a healthy environment in the city than for certain people to be recognized as having "authority." Elders may be those people who have gone before and set a pattern and established a space where Kingdom values pertain, but it does not matter who these people were as long as the space is maintained, and the values internalized by those who now occupy it. This space gives security but this is not for being safe but for taking risks! An example from my own city: youth workers in the city have long had better relationships amongst themselves than most of the church leaders, some of them having grown up together and worked co-operatively for many years. The fruit of these relationships has been that new youth workers starting work in Leeds come into an environment where working together is taken for granted. Some of the longer-established youth workers are in effect eldering youth work in the city. There is no one figurehead leader but a great interplay of gifts, ministries and personalities held together by friendship, by love. Another kind of eldering has come into place as church leaders who have been involved in the establishing of the city-wide Kidz Klub reaching many unchurched children have seen a gap in provision for 11–14-year-olds. They have no intention of setting something up themselves but are looking for something to emerge from what is already going on. One of these church leaders, from one of the biggest churches in the city, started to host a quarterly lunch for all these youth workers, not only to feed them but also to provide a space for them to dream, talk, pray and strategize together. He did this with the full backing of other church leaders and there was *no* sense of threat or suspicion that he might try to exert control, not only because he is known, trusted and loved by them, but because the culture, though strong, is too disparate to be gathered up under one umbrella organization. This church leader exemplifies city eldering. There is no particular benefit for his own church, but he is serving the church across the city and bringing his considerable gifts to bear on a vital area of mission in the city.

If elders in the city are reference-point people who have set a pattern and who provide a sense of order, inevitably a high proportion of them at this stage are likely to be those church-leader-type people who are functioning at a city level. This is probably good for now, as long as they are in good relationship with other church leaders and therefore not seen as being rebellious against existing structures or doing their own thing. Increasingly, we will recognize as elders those people who have opened up Kingdom spaces in the various spheres of the city – for example, education, health, business, voluntary sector, and culture. Eldering will then be more deeply embedded in the spheres of the city in which we are called to be salt and light and will there help express a greater unity/solidarity where it counts – before a watching world and before the powers. Yes, there is a danger that some of these people may try to draw people to themselves and be factional, but there's nothing new in that. Paul, in 1 Corinthians 11:19, sees factions as a necessary evil to provoke believers to grow in discernment. An environment so controlled and safe that factions could not occur would be a worse evil than the one it sought to avoid, and in any case, as we know, would be impossible to obtain.

Summary

The kind of leadership structures we have in congregations and denominations/streams are not transferable to the church in the city where we will be working as fellow laborers with churches and people who are different from us. Instead of hierarchical or "vertical" authority structures we need flat or "horizontal" leadership. The unifying factor is not some visionary leader who can command enough respect, but the vision itself – the vision for the city that comes into clearer focus as others are able to contribute their insights. This process is not held together by "command and control" but by a culture full of Kingdom values – relationship, humility, interdependence, reliance on the Spirit, submission to Christ's leadership, mission, and love for God's people. As existing Christian leaders orientate themselves into this network across the city, it opens up new spaces for entrepreneurial people with leadership gifting to emerge and mission takes the lead. The culture is one where the church is turned inside out, every one of God's people becomes Kingdom-active, and the church becomes apostolic. Ministry gifts are seen as gifts to the Body of Christ in the city to enable it attain fullness of both stature and effectiveness, and not simply as ministers of the congregation. Furthermore, this is an "eldered" culture – it has come into being because people have pioneered it into being and it is nurtured and watched over by elders who have one eye on the church and one on the city. These elders are not appointed or organized – they are the people who are esteemed and have become reference points for the culture.

Note
1. Tom Marshall, *Understanding Leadership* (Sovereign, 1991), p. 144.

Chapter 5

Leadership in the "Church as Fullness"

"The problem with Western Christians is not that they aren't where they should be but that they aren't what they should be where they are." (Os Guinness)[1]

The church that is the fullness of Him who fills all in all[2] is the church that stands through the whole created order. The church as people of God is in view here, not the church in its ecclesiastical structures. The church is not a separate sphere in society but is to fill up all the spheres with the presence of God, calling them to obedience to the Lord Jesus through prayer and declaration, suffering and action. The church, as the agent of the Kingdom of God, is the salt, the leaven, and the light. The end in view is a city without a temple[3] because the presence of God now so fills the city (with the city as metaphor for all of human society) that there is nowhere He is not. The city itself is a force-field of redemption and liberation. This future vision is not a reality wholly divorced from the present reality, but rather by its light we see the present more clearly.

The church is the first-fruits of all that is to come. This amazing and wonderful transformation of human society is brought about by the slow, often imperceptible, working of yeast. "My plea is for the city," writes Henry Drummond. "But I plead for good people, because good people are good leaven. If their goodness stops short of that, if the leaven does not mix with that which is unleavened, if it does not do the work of leaven – that is to raise something – it is not the leaven of Christ."[4] The people of God are the seed of the Kingdom planted in the world by the sower (Matthew 13:24, 37–38). God has strategically placed His children in the world He loves – in families, neighborhoods, work, and networks.

We have become so used to thinking of church as the church gathered, whether in small or large settings, that it is difficult for us to conceive of church as the people of God placed through every sphere. Biblical history shows the innate and sinful tendency of God's people to prefer being gathered together to being scattered. The original blessing on Adam and Eve to *"fill the earth"* in Genesis 1:28, and confirmed to Noah in Genesis 9:7, we find being rejected in Genesis 11:4 as their descendants build Babel. As the children of Israel are about to enter the Promised Land the tribes of Reuben, Gad and Manasseh want to stay where they are, and the beginning of Judges finds the Canaanites not driven out of the land God had given His people. The people of Israel forget the Abrahamic blessing that they should be a blessing to every tribe and nation and come to place their security in the borders of Israel and in their national identity so that God has to scatter them in exile. The Great Commission in Matthew 28 takes up the theme that the people of God are to fill the earth with the gospel of the Kingdom, but it took persecution to scatter the church outside the boundaries of Israel. There is a Babel tendency amongst the people of God – to want to build buildings, to construct something that can reach into heaven and to make a name for ourselves.

> "According to the divine purpose, men were to fill the earth – i.e., to spread over the whole earth; not, indeed, to separate but to maintain their inward unity notwithstanding their dispersion. But the fact that they were afraid of dispersion is a proof that the inward spiritual bond of unity and fellowship, not only the oneness of their God and their worship, but also the unity of brotherly love, was already broken by

sin. Consequently, the undertaking, dictated by pride to preserve and consolidate by outward means the unity which was inwardly lost, could not be successful, but could only bring down the judgment of dispersion."[5]

The unity of the church is essential if it is to be a missionary or apostolic church filling the spheres.

To the organizational mind church scattered may seem far too random, too unaccountable. And yet "surely next to its love for the chief of sinners the most touching thing about the religion of Christ is its amazing trust in the least of saints. Here is the mightiest enterprise ever launched upon the earth, mightier even than its creation, for it is its re-creation, and the carrying out of it is left, so to speak, to haphazard – to individual loyalty, to free enthusiasms, to uncoerced activities, to an uncompelled response to the pressures of God's Spirit."[6] Isn't this characteristic of those born of the Spirit?

You must be born again

We must learn how to be the church in every sphere if we are to see a missionary, or apostolic, church filling up the earth with the knowledge of God. This is a major paradigm shift in our understanding of what it is to be church. This shift may be hard for church leaders who have given most of their time, and exercised their gifting, in the programs of the church gathered and have a great sense of responsibility to keep the environment safe for the people they pastor. Nicodemus must have felt similarly bewildered and frustrated in his encounter with Jesus in John 3. He was a good man, a faithful servant of God's people and of the institutions through which they had expressed their worship. To him Jesus said, *"You must be born again."* This was the only way he would see the Kingdom of God and then enter it. He had to unlearn all he had learnt and start again from the basis of the fuller revelation he now had of who God was. This is not transition but something much more radical and challenging.

In the Garden

Having been involved in church leadership for most of my adult life myself and other church leaders I know have often complained about the way people lose commitment to church programs when they get into their careers, marry and start a family. They for their part have struggled with guilt and been unsure how their now stressed life can be the abundant life Jesus promised. James Thwaites in *The Church Beyond the Congregation* shows from Genesis 1 and 2 that the creation context for humankind was work (subdue the earth), marriage (male and female) and family ("Be fruitful and multiply"). The curse following the Fall disrupted every aspect of this context. The answer of the church from the fourth century onwards was that there was no answer; the truly spiritual life exemplified by the monastic life did not engage with secular work or family life. We have perpetuated the error by positing Christian ministry within the church and its programs. Whilst there has been an abundance of specialist Christian ministry and literature with regard to family life and marriage, until the last few years there has been almost nothing concerning work. I recently went into a fairly large Christian bookshop in a small town in the US. The largest section was devoted to fiction, the second largest to gifts, knick-knacks, posters and music. There were a number of books giving keys to spiritual success in prayer, finances, marriage and parenting but I could find nothing about work. Happily things are changing and there is a growing body of literature and several specialist resources to equip Christians for their work. The fact is that most of our character formation, and therefore discipleship, takes place in the context of our families, our marriages and our work.

Family

Our society is in crisis due to the human and social cost caused by family breakdown. There is a desperate need for the church to be the prophetic people we are called to be and to model a way of being family in the Kingdom of God. We should be advocates for family values and watchful over their further erosion. One young friend told me he believed that, if he and his friends loved their wives, there would be more places for God to inhabit in the city! If we are to resist the pressures on marriage and family we must give attention and commitment to strengthening these things in the Christian community and to developing Christian ministry to families. There is a shortage of gifted Christian marriage counseling but no shortage of couples who would benefit from it. But, even more importantly, we need to see to it that we have the kind of relationships where we can speak the truth in love to one another, to receive it when it comes and to pray for one another. We tend to resist intrusion into our marriages and particularly into the way we bring up our children, probably because we are insecure and know we are not doing a very good job. Some young mothers in Leeds have been meeting together once a month, occasionally inviting someone with more experience to come and talk with them, and they say this is the most valuable way of being church for them, and the fathers are now following suit. These young families who are members of several different congregations also get together occasionally and do church at an appropriate level for the children. These gatherings have arisen spontaneously and not as a church program, and ministry gifts external to the group are called for as required.

Taking work seriously

For the past few years there has undoubtedly been an emphasis of the Spirit on the world of work but there is still a lot to come into place. "Secular" work has been devalued in the church for so long that we have had no theology for work, little understanding of calling and no real idea how to be the church as fullness.

> "The distinction between secular and sacred is a confusion and not a contrast; and it is only because the secular is so intensely sacred that so many eyes are blind before it. The

really secular thing in life is the spirit which despises under that name what is but part of the everywhere work and will of God. Be sure that, down to the last and pettiest detail, all that concerns a better world is the direct concern of Christ."[7]

The mind divided into secular and sacred thinking has been one major obstacle to understanding the place of our work in God's creation purposes; another has been the associated division between the clergy and the laity.

"Most efforts at rediscovering the New Testament vision of every member ministry are half-measures. They focus on the Christian in the church – lay preachers, lay pastoral caregivers, and lay worship leaders. What is needed is a comprehensive biblical foundation for the Christian's life in the world as well as the church, a theology for homemakers, nurses and doctors, plumbers, stockbrokers, politicians and farmers. Recovering this, as Gibbs and Morton said decades ago, would be like discovering a new continent or finding a new element."[8]

There are people who are beginning to find their way on this new continent, others who have been doing so for a long time, pioneering a way for more to follow, and *they are* the leaders. They are probably not recognized as such by church leaders and they may not even be involved in church, as we know it.

A story

Andy, for example, is twenty-eight years old and until recently was a director of a large multinational responsible for developing its sustainability policies across plants on several continents. His role was to improve the company's already good practice in the way it treats the planet, the people who work in it and the communities it affects. He could see the power wielded by large multinational corporations and believed that change in the way they acted could affect the lives of millions of people around the world for good or ill. He discerned the powers at work in and through their structures and saw the potential for improving people's lives. Yet his passion for social justice seemed out of place in churches that had little interest in such issues on Sunday mornings. He grew tired and frustrated by much talk of "revival" which only ever seemed to really focus on numbers of people in church – "more people singing more songs for more time," and prophecies which dealt solely in dramatic spiritual imagery rather than making a practical difference. He was close to giving up on church, and was struggling to understand the value of the church to God.

Turning the role of the church on its head – affirming what people were doing outside rather than sucking them inside – made a major difference to Andy. He was enabled to work out some of his frustrations with the church and to look for more of God in his work. While he was in Leeds, he got to know several other people who took their work seriously as the place of God's calling, and it was exciting to see the mutual stimulation that came about. One context was a small prayer and accountability group where work issues were integral to the agenda of the group; another was a small group of people meeting bi-monthly, again from different congregations, who listened to each other's stories and drew out issues to crunch theologically and pastorally. Each person in the group had a transformational vision for their work although each was working it out in very different ways. Andy has since moved on to a similar role in a larger company, but is now re-energized to connect back into the church and consider how his insights and experiences might be useful to others. In particular, he wants to challenge Christians to be more aware of the web of economic relationships we exist within, all of which have a spiritual dimension because they are built around God's resources. In this area he believes the church has huge potential to demonstrate real lives of economic justice.

(There are other stories relating to those who are firmly positioned in the church "dispersed" recorded in the Appendix 1 at the back of the book.)

Equipping the saints

There are over thirty references to the "one another" type of ministry in the New Testament, and if they were all actually happening there would be very little need for anything else. We need to promote a culture of "one anothering" in and for the contexts in which the saints find themselves. Similarly, we have to recognize that each is responsible for their own discipleship. Jesus calls me to follow Him; it is my responsibility to choose to follow. In church life we have often taken responsibility for people's discipleship at an early stage leading to a culture of passivity and dependence. In the dispersed church it is my responsibility to seek out fellowship and ensure I am not isolated. A friend who has recently returned to full-time university work after a period working as a church leader was delighted to connect with someone else in his department who is similarly trying to work out what it means to be a Christian there. In congregational life we have made a virtue of taking responsibility for others and even absolved ourselves from any responsibility save that of submitting to our leaders. The resulting passivity and lack of independent thought and action is not going to change the world. The parable of the ten virgins in Matthew 25 provides a critique of much of our discipleship in the congregational setting. We get the five virgins with oil to share it with those who have none by putting them in responsible positions. We then try and manage an ever-diminishing supply of oil; the five virgins who had oil end up dry and worn out, and no one has actually got out to meet the bridegroom. This is not to say that we should not make discipleship a priority: in this landscape it is absolutely vital but it happens in the realities of life where the world attempts to squeeze us into its mould, and we learn to live out the countercultural values of God's Kingdom. The model set by Jesus of three years of intensive formation before abandoning the disciples to the Holy Spirit was followed by Paul who spent even less time with brand new believers.

In the quote from *The Call* that opened this chapter Os

Guinness says, "The problem with Western Christians is not that they aren't where they should be but that they aren't what they should be where they are." In the mature church every saint is a leader, an influencer, a responsibility-taker, where God has placed them. No one else can take responsibility for them and certainly not their congregation leader. In reality the flow of ministry has been *from* the saints to the church construct, rather than *to* the saints in their places of mission. The saints take the lead; ministry gifts come alongside to equip the saints. Church leaders may be able to go against the flow and give priority to this kind of ministry, but it is more likely to be other saints who are in similar fields and positions who can share wisdom, experience and insight. Instead of seeing the ministry gifts of Ephesians 4 exclusively as particular people with profile in Christian circles, perhaps we should see them as motivations flowing through the whole Body of Christ from a variety of sources. This kind of ministry is received from those we esteem, rather than exerted by those in positions of structural leadership in the congregation. In fact, it is unlikely that we will find these kinds of people if we only look within our congregation.

Recycled ministry gifts

The gifts and the calling of God are irrevocable (Romans 11:29 NASU), and the significant ministry gifts operating in congregational settings are needed in this new landscape. As indicated, the transition will not be easy and not without some dying! The first step is repentance for our lack of interest in the work of the saints. Our preoccupation with our vision and program has blinkered us to the visions and work of church members. We have primarily seen people in the church context rather than in their family, work or social settings. Then we need to listen to, and humbly learn from people as they talk about their work. During a panel discussion at a conference last year a successful businesswoman broke down in tears when asked how much her church leader supported her in her work, saying that all her efforts to understand and support his vision had not been reciprocated. As we listen and learn, people will begin to gain a sense that their work is of value, and not just their work in church-based ministry.

The small group of business people I meet with regularly, at the beginning called me their "permissioner." By that I think they meant that I gave them permission to believe that what they do in their working lives is the main thing God has called them to, and not something peripheral to the main thing. We need to face up to the reality of power in the church: leaders have power in order to give it away to others. The alternative to this Jesus way of giving power is for power to be taken by rejecting or rebelling against authority; this is neither good for the rebel nor for the rejected leader. "We need a deregulation of church so that people can create in its name."[9] James Thwaites says that whoever gets the name "church" wins against the gates of hell. This name is not the preserve of the church gathered or of its leadership – papal or otherwise – but is given to all the people of God.

The work of equipping the saints for building up the Body of Christ must continue in the dispersed Body, but how might the Ephesians 4 gifts work? As we press into this new continent, people will take many different roads and what works in one terrain will not work in another, but we can be sure that, without these gifts of Christ, the Body of Christ will be malnourished and fail to come to fullness of stature or purpose. There are as yet few stories to tell of it happening, and we still find it difficult to imagine or describe. We lack sight and language, and the words we want to use carry meaning determined by the paradigm we have known.

The network is probably the most helpful organizational structure for the missional scattered church, so how can we imagine these motivations flowing through the network? What hubs and nodes in the network will be necessary to sustain and grow it? What do individuals and communities need to sustain them in their scattered mission? How can we be part of several communities at once without ending up imprisoned in the virtual Christian community? In a network communication is critical – what communications tools can be utilized?

Fivefold ministry gifts

So how might the ministry gifts (i.e. pastors, teachers, prophets, evangelists etc.) listed in Ephesians 4 take their place and fulfill the calling they have to equip the people of God for their works of service, so that the Body of Christ comes to the fullness of its calling which is to fill all things? We have tended to locate these ministry gift people in the context of the gathered church or the organizational structures of the church, rather than "at large" in the Body of Christ in a geographical context. The ordering of the household of God is the work of the elders, rather than the ministry gifts. The relationship between the elders and the ministry gifts becomes crucial to ensure that we move from maintenance mode to mission. In the first-century Jerusalem church elders functioned at all levels from the household to the church in the city. The apostles, as well as teaching in the temple courts to the crowd, went house to house. In other words their equipping gifts were not only used in the setting of the gathered church, but also in the church expressed in and through the pre-existing structures of society – in this case the extended family.

The foundational gifts are the apostles and prophets. Apostles are the big picture people who have one eye on the church as a whole across a territory or demography, and the other eye on the regions beyond which the gospel has still to be taken. They are often not recognized because they are not content to spend their time where the church is already established, but push into areas that others do not see and do not understand. Being misunderstood, they are often insufficiently supported. As foundational people the unity of the people of God is engraved on their hearts. As people graduate from the pastoral and teaching ministries necessary for their grounding and nurture they line up with the apostles so that they themselves become apostolic. We are not going to reach our cities and see transformation in all aspects of the cities' life – social, economic, political, and cultural – without the big-picture strategies that come from apostles. Their function is to ensure that the whole church in the city becomes apostolic. We can then expect to see the apostles calling the church in the city to go and bless other cities, the nation and the nations. They are fixed on the two finishing lines: the gospel to the ends of the earth, and the return of Christ. We desperately need to identify and release these apostolic people. Many of them are unrecognized in our local churches where the pastor-teacher gifts are promoted because these build up the church as institution. Pastor–teachers, who will tend to create safety for the flock, are unlikely to be willing or even able to stand with and encourage the risk-taking apostle. Many such apostles will be obvious – people who start up new Christian initiatives to reach out to the unchurched or to bring the Kingdom of God to bear on fallow ground. Others will be less obvious – they are the entrepreneurs, the people making a difference where they are by exploiting new business opportunities or taking on new challenges. We need to release and support these people and line them up with intercessors so that doors will open for them. The apostle Paul asked for this kind of support so he could exploit the openings he encountered. However, we also know that some of the great city churches of the first two centuries were not founded by the "full-time" apostles, but by apostolic believers who set up businesses there. Paul, Priscilla and Aquila were themselves in business and Paul was able to make enough money to support his team. These apostolic people will be the people who see supernatural breakthrough in their working environments. It will be vital that they learn how to pray to see this breakthrough. The teaching or learning that has got us to this point of maintenance and management of the church, is unlikely to be sufficient for these breakthrough people. A lot of their learning will be "on the job" and they will need a theological grid to test what is happening around them. They are consumed with the task before them and make sacrifices sometimes without even being aware of the sacrificed people they have left in their wake! They need pastors alongside them to ensure that they do not lose their own souls in their pursuit of the goal, and to help them work with others. One of the best things we can do for these people is to facilitate opportunities for them to mix with other apostolic people. There will be synergy when apostolic business people mix with apostolic people working in an explicitly Christian context. Apostles open up new spaces for the Kingdom of God into which others can come to establish the fullness of God's purposes, enabling the apostles to move on to break open more spaces. They are the networkers who can deploy people and resources strategically as exemplified by Paul. He sees a need for Apollos in Corinth, and the strategic importance of the Gentile churches' support for the Jerusalem church.

The other foundational gift of prophet works closely with the apostle. The people of God are a prophetic people. We live in the presence of the future and thereby bring the future, God's future, into the present. Jesus' followers are bringers of hope and challengers of the status quo where it resists this hope. Knowing the truth we speak it in love. We are people who see beyond the present and immediate, and below the surface and apparent. Our ears are attuned to the voice of the Lord who is Savior and Judge and we are obedient to what we hear. We are justice people. The apostle who has the anointing to make things happen must be teamed up with the prophet. The task facing us is too big for us and we need to be able to hear the God-given strategies for making a difference. David as a brilliant military strategist, nevertheless, was totally dependent on supernatural wisdom for the battles he fought. Joseph ended up in high office in Egypt through his and others' dreams; Daniel likewise in Babylon. They were undoubtedly people of great ability but they also knew what it was to depend on God. It is the prophets who discern both what is wrong with what is and what the will of God is. I suspect the vast majority of God's people feel powerless to make a difference and are unable to see what might be. The prophet will equip them to become prophetic by giving them the tools to discern the powers and principalities that govern and are embedded in the structures in which they work. The reason why so many of us find prayer difficult is that we fail to understand the role of the intercessor, which is to stand in the gap between what is and what God wants. If we do not know what God wants, or are complacent and apathetic about what is, we will not become intercessors and God will be inhibited in His action. He has set the world up in such a way that we are His agents and He responds to our requests. I have known people who started to make a note of their prayers for change at work, and were awestruck by the faithfulness of God to answer their prayers.

The pastors and teachers equip the people of God to be apostolic and prophetic. Character, identity and theology are prerequisites for an apostolic and prophetic people. There has been an important shift in our understanding of discipleship. When I became a Christian twenty-five years ago, it was all about believing the right things, or at least not demurring from the right things. It was several years before I understood that God was also healer but by then I had constructed a theology around my brokenness. Now, thank God, many discipleship processes incorporate "encounter" sessions very early on when people are taught that God is their healer. Having got people healed up, we need to teach them that they are children of God, blessed with every spiritual blessing in Christ, joint heirs with Him, with free and bold access to the Father in petition and prayer. They need to come to know the Father so that they get to know what the Father's will is and become true children doing His will on earth. There is a huge pastoral task facing us to help the children of God discover their calling in the world and the way of working it out in line with their God-given personality and gifting. Richard Bolles, author of the best-selling job-hunting book *What Color is your Parachute?*,[10] notes that the careers guidance world is full of Christians! They are pastors to those who are looking for direction. Another pastoral role is that of coaching which is increasingly being seen as more useful than sending people on training courses. Then there is the ministry of lining up people with mentors who can help them at their particular stage of life. In Leeds a former staff member with a national student organization is developing ways to work with graduates through the transition from education to work so that they do not get squeezed into the world's mould. Another friend proposed a monastic-type community for young people going into business to which they could return each night and talk about ways in which their character had been tested that day, take on spiritual disciplines to enable them to be "holy ones" at work, and learn how to pray until they saw breakthrough.

We need to be re-reflexed in our habits of relating. The new covenant is not simply vertical – our relationship with God – but is also horizontal. In this area we have a lot to learn! We need to teach in such a way that our mindsets and worldviews are transformed, no longer conforming to the world's common sense. People need to learn their new family history and identity in the family of God and to learn the way of life in the Kingdom of God. The pre-Christendom church typically took three years over this process. Jesus took the same time with His disciples, which should cause us to question our evangelical pattern of lifelong teaching from which we never graduate. Teaching like that has failed if it does not produce new habits of the heart. We must never stop learning but overmuch teaching deadens the desire to learn and is likely to produce a dependency on the gifted teacher and a disempowering of the hearer. Despite all our teaching many Christians do not have the tools to be able to understand the world and their part in it within a biblical worldview. Biblical stories and precepts take on new life and relevance and give necessary wisdom when applied to situations people face in their working lives. This will often be done best one on one or in small group settings where people are able to talk in depth about these issues. "The New Testament pre-supposes a community in which every person is a theologian of application, trying to make sense out of his or her life in order to live for the praise of God's glory; theology of, for, and by the whole people of God."[11]

Whilst it is always right to preach the gospel, I suspect we are not yet fully in the evangelist's season. Until we are living in such a way that elicits questions and is demonstrating the power of God, the gifts of the evangelists are likely to be sadly under-used. Thankfully Christians are coming out of the ghetto and enjoying more friendships outside of their Christian circles and a growing number are asking how to bring the gospel to their friends ... enter the evangelist. The evangelist's gift is to equip the people of God to be evangelistic and this must be more than learning how to invite someone to Alpha! One of our most urgent tasks is to reinterpret the gospel in post-modernity and to rediscover the gospel of the Kingdom.

Summary

The church as the people of God standing through all the spheres of creation, as salt and leaven, has as her vision the city without a temple of Revelation 21. This is the missional church in obedience to successive blessings and commands to scatter and fill the earth, rather than the Babel church that wants to stay together for security. This is a different paradigm of ecclesiology, not just an amended one and many will need to be born again to see it. The spheres of creation Adam and Eve were to occupy were marriage, family and work. These are not peripheral to the main thing – church-based ministry – they are the spheres in which the church is to grow up. We need to find ways to connect in these spheres and to build each other up. The saints must take responsibility for their discipleship and most ministry will be of the "one another" kind. Ministry gift people presently operating in congregational settings are needed but they must learn a different way of exercising their ministry. It really is about serving and not about leading, and the context is likely to be a network rather than a pyramid-type structure. The five ministry gifts of Ephesians 4 are critical to the maturity in stature and purpose of the Body of Christ and we need to re-imagine them as flows through the network of the city church enabling the church to come to fullness.

Notes

1. Os Guinness, *The Call* (Word, 1998), pp. 166–7.
2. Ephesians 4:10, 1:23; see James Thwaites, *Church Beyond the Congregation* (Paternoster).
3. Revelation 21.
4. Henry Drummond *The City Without a Church* (Hodder & Stoughton, 1988), p. 12.

5. Jamieson, Fausset, and Brown commentary on Genesis 11, Electronic Database. Copyright © 1997 by Biblesoft.
6. Drummond, *The City Without a Church*, p. 23.
7. Ibid., p. 17.
8. R. Paul Stevens *The Abolition of the Laity* (Paternoster, 1999), p. 21.
9. Pete Ward, *Christianity and Renewal*, July 2001.
10. Ten Speed Press, 2003.
11. Stevens, *The Abolition of the Laity.*

Chapter 6

With All Kinds of Prayer

Perhaps the biggest change that needs to take place is found within the areas that Mike has addressed in the last few chapters. A true empowerment of those whose time is taken up within the spheres of our cities is absolutely vital if we are to see our cities impacted at a significant level. This empowerment goes far beyond simply suggesting that the church exists beyond our meetings. It is actually to insist that the church *is* that which is beyond the meeting. The Body of Christ is the church, or to give it an emphasis, the church is Christ in action. So we must lean toward the concept that Christ interfacing with society through His people *is* the church, rather than such an interaction is an action of the church. Of course, it is also true that the church gathers together, but Paul seems to suggest that such a gathering does not constitute the church, but is rather a gathering of the church that already exists as members of the Body of Christ (in 1 Corinthians 11:18 Paul says, *"when you gather as a church,"* in the same way that we can talk of gathering as family, but the family gathering does not make us a family). The church exists in and through all of creation and those that are members of that Body will find themselves coming together. It is to that church that the ministry gifts belong, and it is that church's task to help those who belong to Jesus to mature for the works of service. These concepts being practically outworked are probably the biggest shift that is to take place in the Body of Christ in the Western world over these next few years.

In the book *Gaining Ground* I addressed briefly the area of the church beyond the meeting place, but the main focus was on prayer. It is now to the subject of prayer that I again want to return briefly. Over these past years I have focused mainly on developing strategic prayer, but have also realized that the theology relating to spiritual warfare, demonic bondages and land pollution can be controversial. It is possible to promote unity, but then in the teaching and practice on prayer to undermine the unity that is already present. And it was in relation to that specific problem that I began to consider how best to process the issue of prayer.

Ongoing prayer

Categories are helpful in analyzing, although most categories are inadequate to express what takes place in the flow of life. That will certainly be true in what follows, but I hope that the three categories I am suggesting will at least help to give a framework to develop and release all kinds of prayer in the city in a way that does not undermine unity. The first category I have termed "ongoing prayer." By this I mean the everyday prayers of the individual saints and the corporate prayers of the congregations. If we see such ongoing prayer as the foundational level we will be doing everything in our power to encourage it, and if we advocate any other aspects of praying we will introduce them in such a way that the ongoing level of prayer is not discouraged.

In theory we should get 100 per cent agreement on the need for and the benefit of this type of praying. It is therefore essential that those who carry a mandate to give a lead in a city context, whether that is to lead in prayer or in any other area, continue to find ways to encourage the prayers of the saints. Consideration should be given to this so that no communication on prayer undermines it. We want to encourage the maximum number of people praying in a city. So, as we move on to examine another two categories, we need to bear in mind that we must be committed to encourage the everyday prayer of the saints.

Strategic prayer

The second level of praying I have termed "strategic prayer." I believe that strategic prayer is needed so that we do not simply release more prayer, but that the "more" begins to cover what is often not covered. If we can convince the whole church to pray more, the likelihood is that more of what is already being prayed for will be covered, and that there will be whole aspects of our city that will remain uncovered. I pray for my neighbors, and if I were to decide to pray more it is most likely that I will then pray more for my neighbors. In other words, I will pray for more of what I am already praying for. That is a good thing, but it inevitably leaves many things in our localities not covered in prayer. Strategic prayer needs a measure of shaping, so that the essential elements of the city are covered. Strategic prayer will aim to target the geography as a whole so that the whole geography is covered and not just the areas where the church's presence is strong. It will consider the demography of the city so that all the diverse social aspects are covered. Strategic prayer will look at the institutions (particularly the ones that shape the life of the city) and the positions of influence to make sure that they are covered. It will give attention to the entry points to the city, such as the education and trade aspects, as well as considering the physical entry points, so that they are all well and truly being covered in prayer.

These aspects do not just happen, but are covered as someone, or a team, takes responsibility for this. This is where a prayer strategy is developed. Although I might wish to imagine that the vast majority of believers will agree with the need for such a type of strategy, it is probably only something like 60 per cent of believers who will actually agree. How many will be involved in such a strategy will vary from city to city, but the percentage will likely be considerably less than the 60 per cent that I suggest will agree with the theory. A lack of numbers, though, is not a problem, as I advocate that we do not try and convince everyone but work with those who wish to flow in that direction. Our task is not to persuade but to release the maximum numbers who wish to participate, without discouraging those who cannot respond but are continually giving themselves to the level we have described as "ongoing prayer."

If we present strategic prayer in such a way that it is understood as some superior form of praying, we will soon find ourselves in trouble. If we do not present it as elitist, but rather present it in such a way that it is open to others joining, I believe we can have the best of both worlds. We do not discourage those who cannot "buy" in, but encourage them in their ongoing praying, while we release those who have a passion for strategic prayer. My goal is not to cause competition, but a harmonizing of the work of prayer, so that the maximum numbers are being released to their heartfelt convictions. It is the responsibility of those graced to give a lead to ensure that this takes place.

Other than in a few areas where there might be some small disagreements (such as over praying for those in institutions; praying for institutions to change; praying for the entry points to a city, etc.), what I have suggested so far should not be too difficult to put into practice. A measure of maturity is needed to work toward the releasing of people to their different convictions. It is this issue of release that is the key and the challenge, so some perspectives on releasing the third level of prayer ("prophetic praying") now need to be addressed. I am aware we can hit some controversial and even potentially divisive situations, but it is my conviction that we need to see these people released and released in a way that does not jeopardize the unity in our cities.

Prophetic praying and releasing the watchpersons

First, then, to a definition of what I am including under this term. The terminology might be inadequate but I am using this term "prophetic praying" to distinguish it from the strategic prayer I have outlined above, and suggest it as an inclusive term to cover such prayer activities as: the discerning of spiritual powers over an area; the practice of spiritual mapping; cleansing the land of the effects of historic sin; the making of prophetic declarations, and the like.

I am more than happy to accept that not everyone will be convinced of the need for prophetic praying (as I have defined above), nor for the validity of it. In fact, I am glad that there are those who disagree with my convictions on these subjects, as I am not arguing that such activity is central to the Christian faith. (I might wish to try and persuade people that they are key elements in winning the battle for a territory, but I cannot legitimately argue that they are among the central tenets of our faith.) Strategic prayer is not too controversial, but as there is no universal agreement on this third level of praying it becomes clear that it is this type of praying that presents a major challenge to the unity within a city. However, if we handle this well we can find a way forward that helps us reach a new level of unity – a unity not based on total agreement but on commitment to one another.

In a given set of relationships across a specific geography we will discover that perhaps only 15 per cent of the people will have a conviction about the rightness of such ways of praying. So how do we process the inevitable tension that results? There is (as always) no other way forward than a relational one.

There will be the need for openness and honesty between those who wish to pursue this course and those who are called to give oversight within the geography. We cannot have those who are the prophetic prayers seeking to convince those in leadership of the rightness of their beliefs, but neither can those in leadership insist that the only prayer that is practiced is one that they can endorse or agree with. No one has a monopoly on truth – either at a doctrinal or practical level.

I therefore advocate that those in leadership seek to endorse and release the people with the conviction to their calling, and that those who are called to prophetic intercession do not put themselves above those called to lead. True unity has to be based on the endorsement of each other, not the endorsement of a particular practice. The safeguard in it all is that we hold each other to our first calling, that of seeking "first the Kingdom of heaven." There must be no greater motivation than to see an area impacted for the gospel of Jesus Christ. If those who seek to pray in a particular way are doing so because of their desire to see the Spirit of God come in power to save, then, in all honesty, God will probably even allow for some error in practice to be present. He does not primarily bless right practice but what flows from a pure heart.

These watchpersons are the ones who will be dealing with the spiritual elements over the city, in the sense of discerning what they are, and how they have come to be rooted in that location. In their communication, they should not express any form of superiority, for it is the ongoing prayers of the saints that are the base from which everything else flows. Yet it is also true that what they hear needs to fuel the prayers of the whole church – this simply means again that at the level of communication there is wisdom as to how things are expressed.

We are looking for a unity that is expressed in an even greater level of diversity, with people being released (within scriptural boundaries) to their callings, but with the requirement that they maintain the unity of the Spirit. So in simple terms I suggest the following:

- Honest relationships where no one seeks to control the other party through trying to convince them of their beliefs, nor through exercising disapproval. We are not to make one another in our own image.
- Those those called to lead (or perhaps better, those who are called to create an "eldering" culture) release those who have the conviction to pray in these prophetic ways. Releasing does not require that we agree with every practice, nor even that we understand someone's convictions. We can approve of people without having to endorse their practice. It does mean, though, that we do not criticize their practice.
- Restriction is only introduced when there are practices employed in praying that are *clearly* unbiblical. And by this I do not mean when they are simply in the realm of what I am uncomfortable with. So, for example, I am well aware of the controversy surrounding the rightness, or otherwise, of addressing spiritual powers, but I am unable to see how

(biblically) a person can insist that this practice is forbidden, as there are biblical perspectives on both sides of the argument. Even if one were uncomfortable with it, we would have to be very slow at insisting that it ceased or that we made it an issue of fellowship. Within the bounds of Scripture people have to be released to their convictions, and their convictions might go beyond my *interpretation* of Scripture.

* Finally, that prophetic praying is presented as one more way of praying, and that it is not superior to, nor does it replace, other forms of prayer. In presenting it in this way we are releasing those with conviction to this form of prayer and are approving of them without discouraging at all every other vital form of prayer that is taking place.

If our desire for the city or territory to be impacted is always bigger than our desire for others to agree with our beliefs or practices, then we will not go too far wrong, and even when we find ourselves in tension we will find a way forward. If we can hold through in our differences, then our unity will not be threatened but will even go deeper. We can live with tensions, and sometimes God uses the tensions that surface in our relationships to push us to the place of holding together because of God's acceptance of each other, and not accepting a level of unity that is based simply on a low level of agreement with each other.

So in all the above I am simply advocating that we find ways in which all kinds of prayer can be released, and that it is done in the context of approval. Our cities will not be won when we do everything right or when all our beliefs are correct, but there will be significant shifts when the unity we seek releases the Body of Christ into a greater measure of diversity.

We need all kinds of prayer to be released, so let us make an agreement that we will seek to encourage one another to express our God-given convictions in a spirit of humility. It is easy to criticize that which we do not understand, and sadly criticism can become one more means of control. It was for freedom that Christ set us free, so the spirit of the gospel means we must "err" on the side of release not of restriction.

Before introducing the next chapter there is one more area for consideration.

The Amos-type prophets

Some time ago the Lord spoke to me that it was time for the Amos anointing to be released. This prophet spoke out the word of the Lord, but his main focus was in the realm of issues of injustice. There are prophets who are today speaking into these realms, but sadly there is usually a disconnection between the typical "charismatic" prophets and these people. This is yet another aspect that has to be added to the mix. In our cities there are those with the calling to reawaken the church to her task of being the voice and hands for justice, and the enemy has separated them from those who are praying and those who are discerning powers over the city. The truth is they belong together. Again we will have to find ways of releasing people to their burdens and creating bridges between those of different persuasions, so that we do not force those with one set of beliefs to impose their beliefs on others, but that there is a mutual influencing of each other. These Amos-type prophets are also those who are called as watchpersons, and often are those who are either immersed in, or engaged with, the spheres of the city.

Sue Sinclair writes the next chapter. She is a lady whom I met in the city of Liverpool and was able to encourage the gift that was so evidently within her. She has been used by God to help develop prayer in that context and has often written to me to update me on some new level of answered prayer. I asked her to write a chapter for this book with an emphasis on recounting aspects of her journey. I suggested this, as I believe it is vital to give the practitioners a voice. Good theology is practical, and truth is discovered in action. Sue is someone with convictions, but has modeled so well how to work across a diversity of situations with a spirit of humility. I believe you will benefit enormously from what follows.

Chapter 7

Liverpool – a Gateway City

In 1207 a charter from King John created the Free Borough of Liverpool. At the time it was just a little village with a population of less than 2,000 which had a small fishing fleet and livestock markets serving the immediate area. Mainly as a result of the slave trade Liverpool grew very rapidly until today the wider Mersey region has a population of approximately 1.8 million.

Liverpool is a special place known throughout the world. Its history has been full of bloodshed and death – from being one of the major ports that was used for the slave trade; its support of the Confederates in the American Civil War; its role in the potato famine; its maritime history; its part in two world wars; and, more recently, through the riots of the 1980s, and the Heysall and Hillsborough disasters. It has also known bitter religious divisions between the Catholic and Protestant communities.

Well known for the Beatles, for its football and for transporting millions of emigrants to America, Liverpool is a place of great diversity. It has had seasons of dynamic success and it has had times of desperate pain.

However, God has created the people of Liverpool with boldness and courage to overcome and to laugh through their pain. Always, Liverpool has been full of music and laughter. We have wept together and overcome together. It has also experienced the revival power of God during missions held by the Jeffries' brothers (UK Pentecostal pioneers) and Evan Roberts (the key figure in the Welsh revival of 1904–5) in Bootle during the last century.

Liverpool is a gateway place that even today leads to many regions of the world. That is why it is such an important place spiritually. What happens here will affect the places it leads to, for good or for evil. And God has planned who would live, work or visit this region. The Lord knew who would love the land and the people who would humble themselves and pray and seek the face of God, and turn from their wicked ways, so that then and only then God could hear from heaven, and forgive our sin and heal our land (2 Chronicles 7:14).

God uses ordinary people in extraordinary ways

I never cease to be amazed at how the most awesome God of the universe, chooses to use us mere mortals to outwork His incredible plans and purposes. I have not studied for a theological degree or spent years reading some of the magnificent books written on the subject of prayer. In fact, I would call myself a complete novice. However, what I do not know is shown to me by my Heavenly Father, who knows all things and promises to anoint and equip me for all that He has called me to do.

Born for such a time as this

It all began when I was born again but not filled with the Holy Spirit. I was left feeling frustrated and empty. Something was definitely missing! After a few months I could bear it no longer; I was so desperate for His presence, to know Him as Father, to hear His voice and to know the reality of His power.

One night I had a visitation from God. The Lord was standing on my left and He placed a two-edged sword in my hand. The devil was standing before me and, as I raised the sword, he fled. The Lord said He would never leave me nor forsake me but would always be there for me. Everything that happened was straight from Scripture, but I didn't know that at the time. I awoke filled with the Holy Spirit. Instead of being depressed and frustrated, I was full of joy and peace. As the years have unfolded since that event I have come to understand the implications of what happened.

I am a blessed woman. I have a lovely husband and two brilliant teenagers. We have come through many storms together, and it has been that encounter with God that has always kept me. God is real and nobody could ever take that away from me. I had longed to hear God's voice and to know His presence, and the Lord has given me that gift. Over the years I have grown in my understanding and developed the prophetic gifting God has given me, and have always had a passion for the lost and a desire to see them come to know my wonderful Savior.

The fields are white unto harvest

However, God's Word says the fields are white unto harvest, and yet we, as local believers, were not seeing the reality of that. Why was that? We always prayed and asked the Lord to bless what we were doing. I began to ask the Lord to show me the key.

In response to this request the Lord challenged us to go out into our local High Street and to see things as He saw them. So often we travel around our communities thinking about our families, what we are going to have for tea, or the meeting we have just been to or are going to, etc., and we really don't see things as the Lord sees them.

We walked around the local area and we were devastated at the things the Lord began to show us. He showed us that there was a spirit of death over the area but we didn't know quite what to do about it. In a quiet area not known for trouble, a couple of days later, two men were shot dead in a local gym. The Lord really had our attention and we cried out to Him to teach us how to pray and show us how to deal with this.

A year later the Lord spoke to me about giving up my job and being available full time to work for Him. I started with a clean sheet and not sure what God had planned for my life. However, I began leading Neighborhood Houses of Prayer and encouraging people to form these small groups to pray for their families, neighbors, friends or colleagues. At each meeting we also prayed for a different organization working within our community and during the first month we contacted our police to tell them that we were praying for them.

I began to research our community to help us to pray informed prayers. I looked at the range of ages, housing, employment, crime and health. I was staggered at the results of my research. Local people were dying prematurely from cancers, suicide, strokes and coronary heart disease, and the fertility rate was very poor. Why? There was no logical explanation for the poor health of our community, as there is no local source of contamination to account for it.

Sowing Seeds for Revival – teaching and prophecy

During the summer of 2001, Martin Scott came to the North Liverpool area with a Sowing Seeds for Revival team. Martin spoke about the history of the land, the causes of curses coming upon the land and how to cleanse the land. Suddenly everything began to make sense as we realized the poor health and high death rate were due to the curse upon our land. God had not fallen asleep or overlooked us, but there were serious causes for the curse manifesting upon our people. One of those reasons was that Liverpool was a major port in the slave trade and lots of the main political leaders at the time were heavily involved.

I received two personal prophetic words, which said that the Lord would use me to raise up a mobile school of prayer that would cover the whole of the Mersey region.

Then at a united prayer gathering Martin brought a very strong prophetic word to Liverpool. Speaking of that time as a key moment in the history of our region he challenged the church to get involved in its future. Martin said that it was a pregnant moment in history when the church could begin to shape the city through prayer and action. Restrictions could be placed upon the demonic powers and piece-by-piece, step-by-step into the places of power would come those who would serve the agenda of Jesus. The economics would be affected and that which had not been given to Liverpool before would begin to be released. Where there had been financial and economic injustices, they would begin to be put right because in Scripture, wherever there was a hit on the powers in the heavens above, there were always economic repercussions.

Martin also prophesied that Liverpool would become the Capital of Culture not just for Great Britain but also for Europe. In June 2003 we were selected as the European Capital of Culture for 2008 using *"The world in one city"* as the strapline for our bid. Throughout the region there were great celebrations and the leader of Liverpool Council spoke of a new day where a line had been drawn on the past.

It's time to take back the land

In spring 2002 we started to prayer-walk our community – 162 roads and 5,642 homes. Our community is made up of two areas, Waterloo and Seaforth. I sensed a very major stronghold over the area coming from Seaforth – and asked, "Why, Lord?"

In 1813, John Gladstone had a home built for his family on a site from which he could see the beautiful beaches and sunsets. I looked at the historical maps of the region and discovered that Seaforth was named after Lord Seaforth from Scotland, the father-in-law of John Gladstone. The Seaforth name was associated with bloodshed and murder. John Gladstone himself was a Member of Parliament, a major slave trader and father of William Gladstone, four times Prime Minister of Great Britain. Interestingly, the site of the house and gardens became the very heart of Seaforth. Many years later it was torn apart to make way for a highway. This highway is called Princess Way, but is known as the European Gateway and leads down to the entrance of one of the largest freeports in Europe.

This was the area most affected by poor health, premature death and severe mental health problems. I believed that there was a significant connection between the history of this land and the current situation. We began to pray into this and to seek the Lord about the way forward in dealing with it. We continued to prayer-walk the area and to prepare ourselves for carrying out a prayer-walk around Seaforth.

After much preparation, in September 2002 we prayer-walked the Seaforth area. Three churches walked it together but, before we started, we took communion together as an act of real unity and love for one another. We repented for the death, murder, rape and enslavement that had been part of the origins of Seaforth. We repented on behalf of the church leaders that had accepted slave money for the construction of local churches. We repented that we had not used the authority that the Lord had given us to have dominion over our land. We had allowed the enemy to take territory, which belonged to the Lord. We took back the responsibility as the "Gatekeepers" of the land and declared that from that time on we would be in charge of what would be allowed to come in and out of our land. We believe that something really shifted in the heavenlies over the area that evening.

Since then a new community nursing team has been appointed to help resolve some of the health issues in Seaforth and the area has been awarded funding for regeneration work.

Things happen when we use our authority

Within a couple of months our spiritual authority was challenged with a local community dispute over a decision by the North West Highways Agency and local authority to close one of our roads. I had never been involved in anything of this nature before but knew this to be a dreadful decision, which would be very detrimental to our whole community. We challenged the decision and began a campaign to reverse it. In a period of six weeks the whole thing was overturned and we had our suggestions for improvements accepted. During this time our local councilor became a Christian.

I was invited to apply to become a councilor but knew that wasn't something the Lord wanted me to do. However, an opportunity arose for me to get involved in our local strategic partnership so I applied and was successful. This gives me the opportunity to work with the strategic Directors (Health, Police, Education, Housing, Environmental Health and Social Services, etc.) within my local authority and to be a part of planning the future.

DrugsNET – can God eradicate drugs from our communities?

Ephesians 6:12 says,

> *"For our struggle is not against flesh and blood, but against the rulers, against the authorities, against the powers of this dark world and against the spiritual forces of evil in the heavenly realms."*

We do not need to live in hopelessness. We do not need to allow what goes on in our communities to spiral out of control. As the Body of Christ, God has created us to have dominion. Dominion means "force," "strength," "might," "manifested power," "inherent power," the exercise of operative power," "liberty of action," "authority either delegated or arbitrary," "lordship." If we come before God with clean hands and a pure heart we have the ability in Him to exercise that dominion. As God's children we should be using the power that is available to us through Jesus to shift our communities back to God.

Nobody has an ambition in life to become a drug addict. Addicts have fallen for the oldest deception in the book, "Take this, it's good for you." Satan's tactics never change. However, Jesus died for every person who has ever lived and He has paid the price for his or her sins, just as He has for ours.

Many have seen the amazing scenes in the *Transformations* video telling the story of how God has moved in Cali, Columbia in the battle against drugs. We know that God has no favorites and that He loves the people of Merseyside just as much as the people of Cali. All that was needed was for the church to call on God and obey what He said.

"It's time for the church to arise and to declare a STOP and a turning of this tide of evil." This was a prophetic word from the Lord, given in response to a cry from my heart regarding a leaked letter from the Chief Constable early in 2002 that said, "Merseyside is now the Drugs Distribution Capital of the UK."

Being a practical person I said to the Lord, "How are we going to do that?" The Lord unveiled a very simple strategy and within three days DrugsNET was born. DrugsNET is a network of churches, prayer groups and individuals mobilized to pray for specific targets established through a partnership between Merseyside Police and the Mersey Region Churches. We have been meeting with police officers to establish the specific targets to be prayed about.

Here are some of the targets DrugsNET prays for:

- the young people of the region and the protection of their schools
- the drugs distribution networks e.g. the roads, docks and airports
- the drug gang leaders
- the protection of our police and their families; and for wisdom and insight
- the addicts and those who prostitute themselves to finance their supplies
- those ministering to drug addicts.

There have been many incredible answers to prayer and a major work of bridge-building with Merseyside Police and Safer Merseyside Partnership. We have seen huge seizures, arrests and an increase of resources for our police to deal with the 300 per cent increase in information that has been coming to them. The crime rate is dropping dramatically as the police are having greater success. We believe that this is a key to the transformation of our region.

Other regions in England are also catching this vision and are about to launch DrugsNET in their areas. I have received an award for "Sefton Citizen of the Year 2003" from Merseyside Police and an award from Safer Merseyside Partnership for

reduction in crime and community safety in 2003. Praise the
Lord for His mercy and goodness to us.

Together For the Harvest

The Lord gave me a vision and a prophetic word for our region.
In this vision I saw the ships assembled to go to Dunkirk during
the war. There were ships of every size and shape. As long as they
were sea-worthy and able to carry men, they were used on the
rescue mission. These ships were not intimidated by each other;
nor did they refuse to sail next to another ship because it was
slightly different. They sailed together and had the protection of
the armed forces as they went: had they gone alone, the enemy
would have picked them off and destroyed them. We know the
end of the story: their mission was successful and they brought
the stranded soldiers back safely.

The Lord was saying that this was how He wanted His church
to work together: for the church to honor one another and to
work together when the opportunities arose to bring in the
harvest.

Throughout Liverpool and the Mersey region, the Evangelical
Alliance has a network working across the denominations called
Together For the Harvest. This group is a partnership of leaders,
individuals and churches collaborating together to win a great
harvest of people and to enable the transformation of society.
Together For the Harvest has a dream of a future in which the
people of the Mersey region will repeatedly be given the opportunity to respond to the Good News about Jesus. In that dream
many will respond, and will be incorporated into the One
Church locally expressed. The outcome will be a change in
society – with councils, police, education, health and other
bodies impacted by Christian values. It will also be a time of
increased overseas mission from the region.

This church will be characterized by unity and togetherness of
purpose, amidst a great diversity of styles. We dare to hope for a
time when rancor and competitiveness will be things of the past,
and trust and cooperation become the norm.

In this dream many new churches will be established, and everyone will be living within reach of a significant gospel witness. It will be a time of reduced crime, reduced violence and reduced poverty, with safety on the streets, and strong affirmation of family values. Together For the Harvest truly believes that the Mersey region could become a byword for the penetration of society with the Good News.

In November 2002 I was appointed to the position of Prayer Co-ordinator for Together For the Harvest. We have raised up a team that is now working very hard to see the heavens open over our region. We have started to host Hungry For God prayer conferences, 24/7 prayer, united prayer gatherings called "Heaven on Earth," prayer gatherings into the early hours (often called the "watch of the Lord"), leaders prayer cells and in obedience to 1 Timothy 2:1–2, we are praying for all those in authority.

Merseyfest – the church in partnership

I have been an active member of Together For the Harvest for some years, and in spring 2002 we were challenged to get involved with Festival: Manchester 2003, an event which trained and empowered young people to carry out social action, environmental and crime reduction projects in partnership with Greater Manchester Police, local authorities and communities. Having met as a group of leaders to pray and to seek the face of God about whether we should get involved, the Lord gave us a very clear mandate to go.

God has been prompting us to see the competition, rivalry and sense of inferiority between Liverpool and Manchester broken. Every weekend thousands of football supporters, in both cities, sing songs of hate over each other's teams and cities. Through a number of initiatives both cities are working hard to bless each other and to see the barriers that Satan has erected to divide us, broken down. Manchester City Council even sent Liverpool a Valentine's card in 2003 wishing them well for their bid as European Capital of Culture! Amazing.

The Lord has also spoken to us about launching a major initiative in the summer of 2005: it is called Merseyfest. First, in 2004, we are planning to carry out a pilot project somewhere in the region and then, the following year, we intend to have the full Merseyfest, with work being carried out in each of the Merseyside local authorities. Merseyfest will see thousands of young people from around the UK and the world coming to the region for a week of mission to demonstrate the love of God in word and deed. A similar event took place in Manchester with amazing results, and we are looking to God to transform Liverpool and the region powerfully. Merseyfest is working in partnership with Merseyside Police, Merseyside Fire Service, the local authorities and the communities. We have been overwhelmed by the partners who are coming on board to work with the church to bring transformation to our region. Even a couple of years ago these partners would not have entertained working with Christians.

We are also amazed at the fact that major Christian mission organizations want to be part of Merseyfest. Even in the church Liverpool has been the butt of people's jokes but God has His eye on us. It's humbling to see how God is bringing major denominations and mission organizations to the region to stand with us for the sake of the gospel.

I was appointed as Prayer Co-ordinator for this project and we have launched the Merseyfest Prayer Team, which has been meeting on a monthly basis for some time. This team is made up from members of different churches across the denominations throughout the region. We have really experienced the awesome presence of God in our midst and seen many answers to prayer. We are moving into the Liverpool Cathedral for our prayer meetings, which we know is very strategic, and we continue to be in awe of what our amazing Savior is doing.

Isaiah 61:1–4 is one of my favorite passages of Scripture and tells each one of us that the Spirit of the sovereign Lord is upon us and that we have been anointed to preach good news to the poor, to bind up the broken hearted, to proclaim freedom for the captives and release from darkness for the prisoners, announcing the year of the Lord's favor. Verse 4 says:

> *"They will rebuild the ancient ruins*
> *and restore the places long devastated;*
> *they will renew the ruined cities*
> *that have been devastated for generations."*

This speaks to me of Liverpool and how the church needs to rise up to rebuild the ancient ruins and restore the places which lie in neglect; to renew the ruined city that has been devastated for generations. It speaks to me of the transforming power of God that is released when God's people take hold of His Word and apply it to their land and community.

We are on the victory side

We need to be obedient in the little things that God calls us to, as they line up to make way for the bigger plans that He has. There is a great deal happening in Liverpool and the surrounding region. God is doing something dynamic and we are seeing a huge shift in many areas.

There is much work to be done here and many issues still to be dealt with. However, we are not overwhelmed, as we allow the Lord to guide and lead us one step at a time. Psalm 25:14 says,

> *"The LORD confides in those who fear him;*
> *he makes his covenant known to them."*

We want to be a people who have a reverential fear of the Lord – a people who are so close to Him that we hear His heartbeat – and in whom He can confide. Already we have seen the Lord open the most amazing doors that would have been impossible for us to open in the natural.

Be encouraged in the area that God has called you to. Press into Him for the strategy and breakthrough for the people of your land. Always remember that when things seem their worst, that is the greatest opportunity for God to turn things around and then all the glory goes to Him.

We thank God for what He is doing here in Merseyside. We look to Him for the completion of what has been started. We know that the Lord is going to release a new sound from here that is going to be greater than anything for which the Beatles won acclaim. We want Liverpool to be known as a place where the glory of God dwells.

Chapter 8

Harnessing the Redemptive Purposes of a City

In traveling these past years to cities, a number of things stand out. It does not take too long to realize that every city has a personality. This is something that the biblical worldview simply accepts as a given, hence it was not considered strange behavior to address a city as if it had a personality. So, for example, Jesus spoke directly to Jerusalem as a city with the words, *"O Jerusalem, Jerusalem, you who kill the prophets and stone those sent to you"* (Luke 13:34). Although every place is unique with its own personality, it also becomes self-evident that there are some striking similarities between certain cities. While I consider that there are as many varieties of city-personalities as there are cities, I nevertheless believe that there are only a limited number of types of cities. (In due course I will be suggesting that there are seven basic types of cities.) An illustration that might help is to consider ministry types. There is a ministry gift known as "prophet." All who have this gifting can be called "prophets" or "prophetic ministries." Yet the way they operate in the gift will differ from person to person. They are all prophets, and yet each one is unique. No two prophets will be identical, yet in spite of their differences they are all anointed by the Spirit with prophetic gifts. Although unique, they all belong to the type of ministry we call "prophetic."

My inspiration for the material that follows is from three

sources. The first source was simply that of observation through traveling. There is nothing like experience to help challenge one's theology, and encourage one to find an adequate expression within the biblical narrative to fit what has been experienced. I am persuaded that there are many keys in Scripture that we have not yet discovered. These keys are not at the level of "primary" doctrine, so they should not be used dogmatically in order to divide the church. In writing this material, I am focusing on the very practical issue of seeking to contribute to the breakthrough of the gospel in cities, regions and nations. Nothing I write in these chapters is intended to replace the need of believers both corporately and individually living under the authority of the gospel and being open in sharing their faith with others. So, in using the specific scriptures to help explore and describe the various city-types, I am not implying that this should be the primary way for those scriptures to be read – but I am suggesting that the specific scriptures used are both an ideal point of reference for this exploration *and* also that they deliberately contain teaching on city-types.

The second influence was a set of tapes that contained teaching by Arthur Burke on the "Redemptive gift of cities." This teaching series certainly further fuelled my thinking. I found his teaching foundational on the subject and consider that everyone with an interest in this area would benefit from engaging with that teaching. Arthur uses the motivational giftings of Romans 12 as his basis. However, it has been the seven letters in Revelation (the third source that has influenced me) that has given me the connection and helped me find a way of viewing cities and the call on the church within those cities.

In making an appeal to the book of Revelation I am well aware that a number of readers will be somewhat suspicious! And with good reason, for there is probably no book that has been more abused. For this reason I have outlined my personal journey in the preceding paragraphs and will happily set out my presuppositions below.

Seven letters – seven city-types

The book of Revelation is not an easy book to interpret, except for the first three chapters. Although these chapters are fairly easy to comprehend I suspect that there is a depth contained within them that can be mined over and over again. In *Gaining Ground* I noted that these letters are excellent examples of spiritual mapping (the battles that the churches are engaged in are expressed in the light of the respective city's history and geography), and illustrate so well that either the city will shape the church or the church will overcome and shape the city. Increasingly, however, I have come to believe that we can use these letters at yet another level. They can help us discern the personality of a city and understand the strongholds that are typical in that particular type of city.

In using these chapters in this way, I am not making the claim that I am exegeting these letters in the sense of describing the original intended meaning by the author. I do, however, wish to maintain that what I draw out is also one aspect of the diverse layers of truth that these letters contain.

My presuppositions have developed as I have read through the letters repeatedly, and they have been strengthened as I have been led to apply a specific letter to a particular city as the prayer teams have traveled. Here, then, are my foundational presuppositions:

- What is all-but universally accepted is that in writing to the specific seven churches Jesus is addressing all churches at all times. In other words, these letters to the seven churches/cities are symbolic of the church in all places at all times.
- Although symbolic of the whole, this does not mean that these locations are chosen at random. For the seven cities that are chosen are not the only ones in the area that could have been written to. Indeed, there are some larger cites that are not addressed; hence, I do not believe these are chosen at random. The ones that are specifically chosen I suggest contain specific truth for every subsequent concrete situation.

- The letters themselves are prophetic words to the churches. They contain teaching but the teaching is specifically shaped for each place. This is easy to illustrate in taking, for example, the words to Smyrna and to Laodicea and comparing them. In Smyrna they are told that they are rich, but in Laodicea where they claim to be rich they are told that in reality they are poor. The word given is dependent on the situation being addressed – these are prophetic words. Again the historic and geographic references indicate how the words are shaped for the specific situation.
- Each letter seems to draw from part of the Old Testament story for its framework. Ephesus (the first letter) begins with allusions to the Garden of Eden, whereas Laodicea (the last letter) has allusions to the Exile. The letters in between follow the Old Testament story chronologically. When the whole Old Testament had been told Jesus was revealed. Here in Revelation each church has a story to tell, and I suggest that only when they each tell their part of the story is the whole story told, and the Jesus of chapter 1 can be revealed.
- The cities have different personalities, different gifts, and this requires that the church in that place responds to the risen Christ in a specific way. So, for example, let me suggest that the church in Smyrna can learn from the church in Ephesus, but it cannot be a copy of that church. The church in Smyrna must be the church in Smyrna, not just in a geographic sense but also "personality" or "gifting" wise.
- The New Testament church was united in the city, so Jesus did not write to the church of such and such a denomination in a city, but to the church in that city. By understanding this it strengthens the belief that He addresses the church in that city in order that the city might be impacted. The church was to be the specific redemptive agent for that particular city. The church has to connect with the city in such a way that is appropriate for its specific location. The calling on the church is to impact the city and so must be intimately related to the city. Although addressing the church, Jesus is calling the city to respond by addressing the church. It is not

only that the church belongs to Him but the city, too, is His. Hence, in addressing the church He is addressing the city.

Having laid out my presuppositions, it is time to be a little more specific as to how these letters can be applied.

It is my conviction that the letters to the seven churches in Revelation actually contain significant information about seven different types of cities. The seven cities are symbolic of all cities, but they are more than that – they are specifically symbolic of all cities, with each place being a specific type. These seven prophetic words are addressed to the church within those cities, and they outline both the call on the church in that city and also the specific battles that each place was called to fight.

Apart from the obvious and necessary uniqueness of the particular historical and geographical references, the following aspects indicate how unique each letter is:

* The description of Jesus in the opening greeting is unique (generally drawn either explicitly or implicitly from the revelation of Jesus in Revelation 1).
* The promise to the overcomer is unique in each place.
* The Old Testament history alluded to, is unique in each letter.

Connecting earth and heaven

The church has to connect with the city in which it is planted if it is to reach that place, and this also means it has to connect with the *type* of city where it is planted. The church in Ephesus, for example, is not only to be the church in Ephesus location-wise, it has to be the church in Ephesus personality- or gift-wise. For example, as already stated, the church in Ephesus can (and should) learn from the church in Smyrna, but it cannot copy the church in Smyrna. It has to be the "Ephesus-type" church in Ephesus. Practically, this is why we need to learn from situations all over the world, but need to be cautious about simply importing something from elsewhere.

This is further implied, I believe, by the strange way the letters are addressed to the "angel of the church." In apocalyptic writings it is always best to take the word "angel" to refer to a heavenly being, or, at least, to refer to a counterpart to something on earth. I know that many commentators have suggested that these angels are the bishops or ministers of the churches. But as none of the same commentators seem to claim that the seven angels who blow the trumpets are bishops, nor the four who had been kept ready by the River Euphrates and are to be released are human ministers! It seems best to me to take these references to angels at face value and accept that the reference to an "angel" is actually a reference to a heavenly being. The letters, then, are provoking a connection between the earthly people of God with their heavenly counterpart.

This is a most significant concept. Angelic beings and human beings do not operate the same way. We operate by the grace of God. By definition I can do nothing to make God love me more, and if I were totally sanctified God would not love me any more than He does amidst my imperfections. That is the wonder and challenge of the grace of God. Angelic beings, though, operate by divine commission. They leave the presence of God with a commission to fulfill. Gabriel was sent to Zechariah to announce that he and Elizabeth were to have a child that would be called John (the Baptist). Gabriel could not decide halfway through the delivery of his message that due to Zechariah's unbelief he would simply leave Zechariah and go find someone with greater faith. He had to fulfill the commission given him. He could not return to God having adjusted the commission claiming that the grace of God would cover him.

Although the church operates by the grace of God, if we wish to connect with the angelic effectively we will have to begin increasingly to operate by divine commission. Angels cannot effectively fulfill their task if the church is not lining up with the heavenly commission. The church in Ephesus must become whatever God intends the church in Ephesus to be, if there is going to be a greater effectiveness in warfare, for as Paul says our warfare is not at an earthly but at a heavenly level. If the church does not live by commission and line up with the heavenly beings that are sent to our aid by divine commission, then we will not be as effective as we could be.

I believe one of the primary roles of prophetic and apostolic ministry is to help the church in the city to align rightly with the heavenly messengers that are commissioned to help it, so that we become as effective as possible. If a divine connection gives us an increase in effectiveness (God-connections yield a fivefold increase according to Leviticus 26:8), then I am asking the question as to what might shift very quickly when the church truly partners with the angelic. Hence, it is vital that the church in a given city is the church God intends for that city (a church living under divine commission) so that it effectively participates in the advance of the Kingdom.

In *Gaining Ground* I recount how I had a vision one day in Wales of both stationary and all-but stationary angels. It was then that I realized that these angels had left heaven to fulfill a commission over Wales and that many were still at their post as the commission had not yet been fulfilled. They were waiting for the church to rise again and partner with them.

I have a very good friend, Rich, in California who is a pastor of a church. He also has a most remarkable gift in the realm of prophetic dreaming. However, the way the dreams operate is a little unusual. As Rich dreams he normally enters into a dialogue with whatever is going on in the dream in such a way that his side of the conversation can be recorded. One night on a retreat he was sleeping in the same room as one of his sons. In the night he began to dream and to dialogue. Not only that but he began with some energy to move his arm in a continual large arcing movement. Back and forth the arm went, until the movement and the conversation ended with an instruction to "remember to shut the door when you leave."

In the morning Matthew, his son, asked his father whether there had been anything unusual about the night just gone. Rich said nothing that he could remember, but that he had obviously slept awkwardly as his whole arm was aching! With a few more questions it wasn't too long though until the dream came back to Rich. He explained that an angel had come to him in the night saying that the flames of God were present in California but that they needed to be fanned to a new level. To do this the angel was ready to take one side of the bellows but that nothing effective would take place without the church taking her side of the bellows. God's bellows only operated as the church and the angels partnered. In the dream Rich had enthusiastically grasped hold of the other side of the bellows and begun to partner with the angel – hence, the arcing arm movements.

This certainly explained the movements and the conversation. Matt was, however, intrigued by the "remember to shut the door when you leave" line. Rich explained that there was an element of angelic activity that could be annoying. He said it is not good when they show up, leave by the door, but do not shut the door! On this occasion he said he wanted to make sure he got in early with the instruction so that the angel had no excuse!!

Whether an angel leaves a door open that we would rather have had shut is fairly immaterial, but what is essential is that the church partners with the angels, and to do so it is important that the church in the city discovers what it needs to be in that location.

This need for partnership, or perhaps better put, to be harnessed to the angelic is expressed both at the death of Elijah (by Elisha) and at the death of Elisha (by King Jehoash). Both times the cry is, *"My father! My father! The chariots and horsemen of Israel!"* (2 Kings 2:12 and 13:14 respectively). As a major prophetic figure is departing, one of the burning issues is what will happen to the armies of heaven. With the departure of Elijah the armies of heaven are still connected to the people, but with the death of Elisha I suggest that the connection becomes very weak. Prophets who are called to stand in the presence and counsel of God are there to help the church connect with the angelic beings who also stand in the presence of the Living God. As fellow-servants of the one true God the earthly and heavenly messengers are to partner, thus causing an acceleration of the purposes of God and a fanning of the flames of God's revival fires.

The types of cities

It is not an easy task to describe the different city-types succinctly and I am also aware that other writers would wish to utilize different descriptions. The names I have chosen to use as descriptions of the different city-types are based either on the part of the Old Testament story that the letters allude to (as in the case of Ephesus, Smyrna, Pergamum and Thyatira) or on the internal gifting of the city (as in the case of Sardis, Philadelphia and Laodicea). To some of the cities I will also give a second name as they carry more than one aspect of gifting, and their giftings are not always adequately described by one phrase.[1]

Ephesus: a first city
The allusions here are to the Garden of Eden, for overcomers are promised that they will eat of the tree of life in the Paradise of God. I suggest that this type of city is a place where it is easy for things to be given birth to, where, for example, events, projects, organizations, etc., can begin. This is the essential and unique gift that these places have to offer.

Smyrna: a deliverance city
The people of God are experiencing extreme opposition here and the expectation is that it will actually become even worse before it gets better. However, the promise is of deliverance. The allusions here seem to be to the Exodus. So this is a place where testimonies of God's deliverance will be discovered – but only as a result of persevering through hardship.

Pergamum: an establishing city
The allusions here are to the wilderness and the conquest (we read of references to Balaam and to hidden manna). The purpose of exiting Egypt was to enter the land. The danger in these places is of succumbing to the temptation to wander, rather than fulfill the goal of entering the Promised Land. I call these places "establishing," as it is vital that the people of God do not wander but begin to establish the promised inheritance. At their best

they can take what has been done elsewhere and move those things forward, while at their worst they can stand in judgement over the prophetic word of the Lord and claim to have God's favor on them while in reality they are simply wandering in the wilderness.

Thyatira: a model city

The promise to those who overcome in Thyatira is that they will rule the nations; the opposition is described as being from "Jezebel," who usurped the authority of the kingship in the Old Testament, and was a major contributor to the establishment of false worship in the kingdom of Israel. So the Old Testament allusions are to the days of kingship. The establishing of the earthly king was at best a mixed event, and at worst it was an outright refusal to accept the Kingship of Yahweh. However, the Lord was willing to accept the kingship, particularly as manifested under David, as an earthly model for the Kingdom of God. When rulership goes wrong, it is abusive and restrictive, yet it is the term "kingdom" that was on the lips of Jesus to describe the order that He was initiating. Hence, I choose the term "model" for this city.

Sardis: a city of mercy

Allusions to a specific part of the Old Testament story are not as clear in this prophetic letter as in the other six. The practical instruction to "wake up," though, can be seen as rooted in the wisdom literature – the literature that chronologically came as a result of the establishment of the kingship, with much of it written or collated by Solomon. Sardis was a city that was exceedingly tolerant and where there was to be an abundance of the Spirit's presence. For these reasons I suggest that we have in Sardis a city that is a city of mercy, displaying the characteristics of the mercy of God.

Philadelphia: a gateway city

Philadelphia had an open door set before it. Its purpose was to go forward and expand Graeco-Roman culture into new territory.

Hence, I am using the term "gateway" as a description of this city. We read here of allusions to the building of the Temple and if there is a response to the open door of mission, Jesus makes the promise of His presence being among them. The establishment of the Temple of the Lord throughout the earth is particularly linked to that of mission.

Laodicea: a giving city

Laodicea was exceedingly wealthy and as such was called to be a giving city, not living in independence but ready to be a supply where others were in need. Ephesus began with allusions to the Garden of Eden, but in Laodicea Jesus comes as the origin of all creation. The beginning of the story is one of a garden, but the end of the story is to be one of harnessing all of creation's resources for the purposes of God. So I suggest that Laodicea is not just a giving but also a finishing city. The allusions in this letter are to the Exile (being spewed out of the land/being spewed out of the mouth of Jesus), so the danger is of losing one's territory and the challenge is to see the fulfillment of the purposes of God in creation regardless of external circumstances.

The table below summarizes the material thus far:

City	Type	Old Testament allusion
Ephesus	A first city	Garden of Eden
Smyrna	A deliverance city	Exodus
Pergamum	An establishing city	Wilderness/conquest
Thyatira	A model city	Kingship
Sardis	A city of mercy/development	Wisdom literature
Philadelphia	A gateway city	Temple
Laodicea	A giving/finishing city	Exile

There are a great many patterns in the book of Revelation, with most of them centering on series of sevens that are often then further subdivided into threes and fours. It seems that these letters, too, are patterned in this way. A number of scholars see a pattern (known as a chiasmus) that indicates Thyatira is at the center, thus giving further weight to the concept of that city being a model for others to see.

This pattern that places Thyatira at the center not only suggests that what takes place there is to be a model (not a blueprint) to other places, but that Thyatira-type cities will draw up into themselves characteristics that are manifest in the other six-city types. By using the term "model" I am not implying that Thyatira is greater than anywhere else – indeed, the city of Thyatira was the smallest and perhaps the least influential of the seven cities in Revelation. Further, by using the term "model" I am not suggesting that other cities cannot produce models that can be learned from.

Another way to signify this pattern and to emphasize how a model city draws aspects of the other cites up into itself, would be to lay it out as shown in Figure 1.

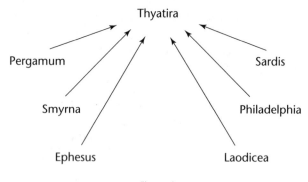

Figure 1

City-types – some clarifications

If a city is of a certain type, this does not mean that the only gifting that will be manifest in the church in that city will be the gifting I have described. An example from everyday church experience will illustrate this. Suppose individuals have the gifting of prophet, this does not mean that they cannot also evangelize and share their faith – it simply indicates that their *primary* gift is that of prophecy. Likewise, if a church as a whole has a teaching anointing, this does not mean that there will be no prophets, evangelists, or pastors within that church. So, by defining a specific gift for a city I am suggesting that that particular gift will need to be clearly manifested, regardless of whatever other gifts are developed.

It also means, though, that if the church in that city does not discover and flow in its primary gift, it will be very difficult for that particular city to be harnessed for the purposes of God. Even if other gifts are manifested, but the critical gifting is not, it would be most difficult for a breakthrough to be experienced. Hence, these categories should help bring focus and enable the church in the city to prioritize.

Another aspect that we will pick up later is where we discover a city having the same gifting as the nation has. (This might be the capital city of the nation, but this is not always the case.) If the cities in the nation that carry the same gifting as the nation can break through, then the nation will come through to her purpose much quicker; conversely, if those cities do not break through, it will be very difficult to get a clear breakthrough in the nation as a whole.

Cities – the basic pattern

- Jesus comes with a specific greeting. How He reveals Himself to the church is how He wants them to know Him. The church has to receive Him in the way that He comes to them. What He reveals *to* them is what will be revealed *through* them. In the opening greeting from the risen Christ there will be some indications of the gifting that is to be manifest.
- In the course of the letter Jesus picks out where they have succumbed to the pressures that are within their city, or He picks out aspects for which the church is to be commended. The former areas are descriptions of where they have come under the specific demonic strongholds that seek to ensnare their city; the latter areas indicate the strongholds to which they have not submitted. Either way we gain an outline of the typical strongholds that this type of city has to battle against.

- He gives each church/city a promise that relates to the age to come and will be fully experienced then. However, the calling on the church is to show in the here and now what is to come, so we can see from the promises specific characteristics that are to be nurtured in the city. These promises fully manifest in the age to come will be partially (and significantly) manifest in this age – when the church is living under the specific heavenly commission.
- We can also gain some understanding concerning the purposes and calling on the particular city through paying attention to the particular aspect of the Old Testament story that is alluded to.
- Outside the scope of these letters (and an area that I will not develop within this book), but drawing on the teaching and experience of Arthur Burke, there is the discovery of "the catalytic institution" that needs to be connected with in order to see a breakthrough catalyzed. These institutions, for example, can range from church to business, from family to government. The specific catalytic institution is often the means by which the city came into being, grew, or gained significant momentum. Through specifically engaging with these catalytic institutions, Arthur suggests we discover how best to release the specific birthright of that city. By the term "birthright" is meant the absolute unique contribution that city is designed to make.

Drawing from the above points we understand that there are general truths for all cities but that cities can then be subdivided into seven types, so we can say, for example, that not all cities are "first" type cities. Then, within the category of "first" city, not all cities will have the same catalytic institution that should be engaged with to gain the maximum effect in the shortest period of time. And, finally, each and every first city will have a unique contribution to make: that is their birthright.

The further we take the process, the more specific and unique the identity and purpose of the city becomes. However, given that the primary definition begins at the level of discerning the type of city we are wanting to impact, that will be the focus of the following chapters. Once that has been discerned and work has begun on the strongholds over the city, it will often become apparent what institutions will specifically need to be engaged with, as they will frequently be the area under severe attack or even bondage.

Some other comments

Each of the comments below could be expanded somewhat but a few headlines for now will suffice. I also suggest that there might be value in returning to these headlines after completing the subsequent chapters on the city-types.

Each city has its own gift but this will be modified in at least three ways:

- Each city will draw gifting from the two cities that are placed either side of itself in the sequence. (As mentioned already Thyatira goes further than that and draws gifting from all other six cities.) So a city of mercy will also carry giftings related to a model and a gateway city. Hence, in discerning a city it will be important to take note of the cities that are positioned either side. (As Ephesus and Laodicea are at the ends of the set of seven I need to explain that Ephesus has some of Smyrna and some of Laodicea; likewise, Laodicea has some of Philadelphia and some of Ephesus in it.)

1. National/regional gifting will manifest at a measure in the city gifting.

2. A city with the same gifting as the nation must come through to help the nation through.

Figure 2

- Second, each city will also carry some of the gifting of the nation or region where it is planted. So, in looking at the gifting of a city, there also needs to be some consideration of what is the gifting of the wider region. (See Figure 2.)
- In defining the cities as I have, I am presenting these as tools to help unlock the locality. If we use the analyzes as tools we will find them useful, but if we try to make everything fit rigidly we will probably be frustrated. Just as with an individual, the gifting in a city will also be affected by history. The gifting could well be perverted through what has happened (and this will certainly be true in measure until the church begins to act redemptively) or the gift could be suppressed through past experience. As the city is impacted spiritually, the historical experiences that have laid a negative layer over the city will have to be addressed.

Hence, given that the gift of the city is modified in these ways, the following chapters are not intended to present a simplistic solution to discerning the gift of the city, but to be a grid that with discernment and research will further aid us as we seek to harness the places where we live to the purposes of God.

Given that Thyatira divides the other six cities into two groups of three we will find that in an area or a nation that has a particular gifting there will be a predominance of cities that sit in that pattern of three. (The two sets of three are: Ephesus, Smyrna and Pergamum; Sardis, Philadelphia and Laodicea.) So, if the region has a gifting of Smyrna, for example, there will tend to be more cities that belong from that set of three than from the other set of three.

In the pattern of two sets of three we will also note the close correspondence between the cities and the order they are presented within those two sets. Thus, the following pairings will have strong similarities to each other: Ephesus and Sardis; Smyrna and Philadelphia; and Pergamum and Laodicea. From Ephesus to Pergamum something is to be established in the land, and from Sardis to Laodicea something is to be harnessed from all creation. Smyrna and Philadelphia will often find themselves being squeezed as they seek to release what has begun either in Ephesus or in Sardis. As these patterns are developed there are many possible combinations that will prove helpful. Here I outline just three for consideration:

* Different types of cities can help one another – so that the different gifts and callings can complement one another. This is why it is necessary for cities to relate rightly together.
* There will be specific ways in which combinations will work within the patterns of three. First places will need to partner with deliverance places in order to help bring establishing places through. Places of mercy will work with gateway places in order to release giving places.
* A city with a particular gift will be ideally gifted to connect to a nation with that same gift. I believe a person breaks through in order that a church can break through; a church, in order that a city can break through; and a city in order that a nation can break through. If I, at a personal level, can testify to a specific breakthrough, it is a strong encouragement to faith for those held in the same bondage, and this pattern works all the way through the above examples. Once a city breaks through there is a testimony for the bigger unit under the same bondage – hence, a city connecting to a nation with the same gift (and therefore being under the same type of strongholds) will help that nation break through.

Another important facet to the understanding of cities should also help not only to bring focus but also perspective. Just because, for example, a church in a particular city is under extreme pressure (Smyrna-type), this does not necessarily mean that it is missing its way. Indeed, in such places God desires a breakthrough that will become foundational for elsewhere. Often in those places – as opposed to the more "successful" places – God desires to raise up strong apostolic works, for they often understand the true nature of ministry as servanthood.

Suitable diagrams?

I have often tried to illustrate how the cities might interact together and sought to use diagrams to portray this. Inevitably, whatever diagram is used will always have limitations, and it is vital to demonstrate that there is no hierarchy of cities, but there is the need for each one to play its part. This can mean, though, that one city will have a greater part to play at a given time than at another time. However, any "greater than" aspect is only temporary, for the fullness that Christ desires to be manifest will only come as unity and partnership arises between cities.

I am convinced that in due course there will be revelation showing the interaction of cities in specific ways, and also how the spheres of society fit to play their part. Let me first suggest that there could well be a connection between the cubic manifestation of the New Jerusalem and the seven typical cities of Revelation.

The book of Revelation takes us from chapter 1 where we are presented with the fullness of the manifestation of God in the risen Christ to the closing chapters where the fullness of God and Christ is resident in the New Jerusalem. The middle chapters are all about the warfare between the saints of God and the enemies of God, which are preceded by the letters to the churches in the seven cities. The churches are called in their settings to manifest their part of the fullness of the risen Christ. If the churches are not successful, then there will only be a manifestation of the Babylonian city that rises up from the earth. In truth, the church will be successful in part, for it is only when the New Jerusalem comes down from heaven that the completion of its calling will be made manifest. All that could have been revealed will then be finalized, with the kings of the earth bringing their glory into the new city.

This six-sided city, the Bride of Christ, is destined to rule (the promise to Thyatira, the model city). The cities are to manifest an element now of what will be fully manifest then in that heavenly city, with the rule of God being expressed through the cities in six distinct ways, yet with that rule only being complete in the inter-relationship between them all. In using the illustration of the New Jerusalem each city would represent one face of the cube, with Thyatira filling the space between the cities, modeling something of the whole. The New Jerusalem, then, is to be made visible (in part) in every city as the church redemptively takes her place, and in turn the New Jerusalem is the fulfillment of what has been taking place in every city that has been responding to the call of God.

The only other time we read of a cube in Scripture is with reference to the Holy of Holies, so this must be the challenge before every church – to manifest the presence of Christ within their city. We might even suggest that the book of Revelation is a tale of two cities: the Babylon that seeks to rise up and the Jerusalem that graciously comes down. If every city can harness its potential and allow the Jerusalem that is above to invade, then our great hope is that the riches from within every city, and indeed every nation, can flow into that final city. This then is our call – let the church rise in every place and connect with heaven, so that the heavenly city that one day will be manifest might in measure become visible in the here and now.

In Figure 3 I outline a second approach. (Once the following chapters have been read the comments in the diagram will be

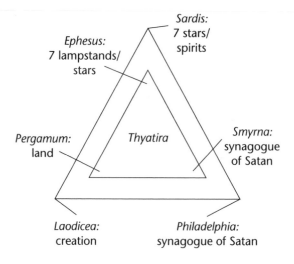

Figure 3

understood.) The diagram illustrates that the first three cities relate together as do the last three; and that the last three are an expansion of the first three. There is a very real correspondence at the corners, seen in the descriptions that I have highlighted. It also illustrates that if, for instance, a first city cannot find a deliverance city to relate with, then it is equally possible for this to be a gateway city.

Given the framework that I have set out in this chapter it is now time to look at the individual letters in more detail. In the following chapters I will follow the order that the cities appear in the book of Revelation, with Thyatira sitting in the middle of the two series of three cities. Every city is vital, for only when each one comes through to its destiny and relates to the other places will there be a fullness of the revelation of Jesus.

Note
1.   Appendix 2

Chapter 9

Ephesus: City of Firsts

(Revelation 2:1–7)

Ephesus was a most significant and impressive city.[1] The architecture was something to behold, with one of the seven wonders of the ancient world, the temple of Artemis, within it.

In referring to it as a "first" city, I do not mean that this type of city is the most important, or that they are the ones that are to rule over the others. I do mean, though, that they are called to give a lead, to go on ahead, to be initiators and to pioneer. If called to pioneer, mistakes will inevitably be made and there will be some testimonies of failure that come from this type of city. So, by first, I mean that these cities are called to break new ground.

The city of Leeds, about which Mike Love has already written and into which the prayer teams I am associated with have invested quite heavily, is without doubt a first city. I am writing these opening paragraphs while there, and it has amazed us over the past few days how many firsts are in the city. Even when, for example, they began a "kidz klub" style work among unchurched kids, although it was not the first kidz klub in the world nor even in Britain, it was the first one in the UK (and as far as we know in the world) where it was initiated, run and supported across a number of churches from the city.

It is a privilege to give a lead, but there is also a pain involved in doing that. The pain of starting more than is finished, of seeing others do it much better and improving on what was prototyped, and in particular the pain of being misunderstood: these all go with the territory of being "first."

So, with these comments serving as an introduction to first cities, it is time to look at the prophetic word to the Ephesian church.

Jesus comes to a first city

He comes as the one who holds the seven stars in His right hand, who walks among the seven golden candlesticks. Each and every greeting to the seven churches is unique, but there is a particular area where the greeting to the first city is different from all the others. It is only in the greeting to this letter that the symbols used are ones that have been previously explained. Chapter 1 is full of imagery, most of which is not explained. The only explanations are given at the end of the chapter where the seven stars and the seven golden lampstands are interpreted. So there can be no debate as to what they mean.

A first city is a place where things need to be made clear. There should be very little room for misunderstanding. Because these cities have a gifting to begin things, then it should not be surprising that there has to be clarity of understanding in them. With the symbols we are to work out what other symbols can mean by taking our cue from what has already been explained, so that by being clear over these symbols we can work from there and begin to see what other symbols might mean. In other words, if we can start right we can go forward from there, whereas if we start wrong it is going to be increasingly difficult to get back on line. So in first cities God wants to release patterns that can be followed – and even improved on. What is experienced in first cities (good and bad) is intended to help us make sense of what is going on in other situations.

First cities, then, need to be places where communication is clear. Where there is no confusion over what God has said. The prophetic word into these places is vital; for something can be released there which can serve to help other cites to take their cue from that. The Sowing Seeds for Revival teams that I have given a lead to "accidentally" began with two weeks in the city of Leeds, and then that city was the first city we visited every January in subsequent years. I did not understand the nature of first cities until our most recent visit to Leeds, but have always discovered that what we experienced there would then be released into other situations for the following six months or so. Each year we have always discovered something new there. I now understand that this is part of the redemptive gift of first cities.

Paul's visit to Ephesus lasted for just over two years and we read that as a result there was communication of the gospel throughout the whole of Asia (Acts 19:10). There were, of course, practical reasons for such a successful level of communication, but there is also the sense that this type of city can become a center for communication.

This is normally the case in the physical realm too. One such first city in the UK has significant television and radio stations, which broadcast not only regionally but also nationwide and even internationally. That city also has significant publishing houses and currently something around 65 per cent of UK Internet traffic goes through it.

Some central characteristics

Although city-types need to be spiritually discerned, given that the material and natural realms speak of and reflect spiritual realities it is not surprising that there will be some visible and discoverable specifics that will indicate the presence of the gifting of a "first city." Some indications will include:

- a history or reputation of being one of the first to do something, so it will be a place of innovation
- a place of communication, often with a significant media presence, or where the university has a leading media studies department
- impressive and ostentatious architecture
- a significant economic presence

- areas of significant deprivation that (until the city begins to turn) are ignored
- ideologies birthed that are propagated and held to dearly.

Jesus comes to the first city in such a way that there is a deposit here for all cities, for He comes holding the *seven* stars and walking among the *seven* lampstands. Those stars and those lampstands represent the whole, so Jesus comes to these places to assure the church that the destiny of the church (represented by the seven stars in His strong right hand) and His presence among the church is intact. So, if ever there should be a place that has a spirit of faith and lives from a heavenly destiny, it should be a first city. From these first places there should be a flowing of the prophetic word to the churches of their land to lift their eyes and know the Jesus who is on the throne.

Prophetic gifting needs to be part of the church in such cities and the prophetic gifting that is released will be to help align the earthly church (represented by the golden lampstand) with their heavenly counterpart (their star or angel).

Surface strongholds

At this stage it is fairly easy to understand some of the strongholds that first cities will have to deal with, for the enemy will seek to pervert the true gift and lock it up from the people of God. Indeed, one can make a quick judgement as to how free a city is by considering how free the church is to move in the inherent first city gifting. If there are no firsts taking place in the church, then we know that the city is not very free. So we can summarize some of these early strongholds as:

- No firsts taking place in the church and no spirit of adventure or entrepreneurship manifested.
- Communication problems among the Body of Christ, particularly where plain things become confused.
- Strong opinions keeping the Body of Christ apart.

- Accusation from the enemy that the believers have nothing to give beyond their city. Given that the city will begin more than it finishes, there can be a strong sense of inadequacy. This will often also be accompanied by "together" places being very critical of what is going on in a first city because it is not impressive! Indeed, the enemy will even cause rumors to be spread about what is happening in such places, for from the enemy's perspective the voice of the first city must be silenced at all costs. If the starting place is shut down or even just slowed down the work of God in a nation will be seriously hindered.

- An over-focus on finishing and a corresponding reticence to begin something. Although there is no virtue in starting without finishing, in a first city it is a sin not to initiate. The gifting to finish what has been begun might not be too present, but as one city after another comes on line there needs to be faith that in the right season there will be help that flows to the city to aid with the finishing process. (Ironically in a first city there is also a measure of finishing gift, as each city draws up into itself something of the gifting to either side of it. I will explain how this comes into operation later in this chapter.)

A twinning gift

Given that a first city has a gifting to initiate and start, and also because a first city carries something of a mandate for the whole church (represented by the heavenly and earthly "sevens" in Jesus' greeting), there will be a strong gifting to twin with other places. It is vital that new things begin and old things that are stuck are kick-started to a new level. Hence, I suggest that first city gifting means that other cities need to call for their help to ensure that there is continual movement.

It is vital that a spirit of humility covers those who work from a first city. "First" is not to mean "above" but "before" in the sense of being willing to go ahead, to make mistakes and get the bloody nose first. The use of the term "first," though, does imply that these places do need to come back with news that there is a way forward, that there is ground to possess that has previously never been touched, that there are way of doing things we have not thought of before. These first cities need to be willing to make themselves available to other cities even when they don't have all the answers, for their infectious faith can open up new possibilities and by the grace (and intent) of God other cities might then be able to go even further than those first cities.

Enemy strategies

In this prophetic word to the Ephesian church Jesus rebukes the church in one area and strongly commends them in two areas. This indicates there were three key areas in which the enemy could ensnare them so that their destiny would not be fulfilled. In the church in Ephesus, as recorded in this chapter of Revelation, they had done well on two of the areas but had failed in one aspect. So alongside the obvious surface strongholds there are three areas of life that have to be safeguarded above all others. Those three highlighted in this prophetic letter are:

- protection of the church against introduction and establishment of false apostles
- a refusal to be complacent about the Nicolaitan heresy
- the importance of holding on to their first love.

So seeking to look at these one at a time, let us take them in the order that I have laid out. Paul had previously warned the Ephesian elders that, when he left, "savage wolves" would come in to devour the flock, and that some of those destructive leaders would even arise from within their own company. A key element in discerning these savage wolves, Paul says, is that they would entice disciples to become personal followers (see Acts 20:17–38).

In a first city, where there is to be innovation, it is vital that anyone gifted to give a lead does not rise up to become above others, producing their own following. As the city begins to develop there will be a desire to minister in it. It will draw ministry gifts to it (and so it should, for true apostolic ministry needs to come to a first city and partner with it) but the danger is of apostles developing their own disciples and even their own churches in such a place. Apostles do not own churches; rather apostolic ministry belongs to the churches. Whoever the apostles are, Paul says they all belong to the church, and not vice versa (1 Corinthians 3:21–23).

It is key, then, that there are overseers who will take responsibility – indeed, it was to those people that Paul addressed himself in his farewell speech warning of dangers ahead. Who are the ones who should take responsibility? I suggest that at times even the wrong ones need to take an oversight role! Let me explain. In the early stages of a city developing it is rare that all the right people are in place, and it is at this stage that God is looking for someone to stand in the gap until others are in place. It is simply vital that some people humbly, and with a measure of recognition, step forward to take responsibility. It might be in due course that they will give way for others, but if they can begin on a path with great humility they will have opened up a way for others to follow in similar humility.

There will come a stage as the church in the city begins to move forward that apostles will need to come into place. Prophetic ministry can open up new areas through the spirit of revelation, but it is apostolic ministry that can then begin to lay foundations as to what this means for the gospel. The message of the gospel cannot be changed. That has been delivered once and for all from Jesus through the apostolic church, and in that sense the twelve were unique, and even Paul did not belong to the twelve. He had no authority to change the gospel, but did have an authority to work out in God what the implications of the gospel were in a new context. This is apostolic work and, in a first city where the gospel will be expressed in new contexts, apostolic ministry will be essential.

A major mark on those who carry true apostolic ministry for a first city will be that they are those who come to serve and do not draw disciples after themselves. They will be those who come to dialogue and to learn, as much as they come to impart. They will not come with their preconceived ideas, but drawing upon their wisdom and experience will be able to see it expressed in new ways in an ever changing and moving situation. They will be those who willingly identify with the city and all its failures, being ready to work across a diversity of church expressions.

The second area where the Ephesian church had done well was in "hating the works of the Nicolaitans." There is considerable debate about what the Nicolaitan heresy was, but given that one of the central themes of the book of Revelation is that of overcoming and that the name "Nicolaitan" is a play on words being made up of "overcoming the people," it seems most likely that we have here a description of a movement, a tendency, or a spirit of ruling over people. This is in contrast to Jesus who through His meekness overcame the enemy in order to release the destiny of people. It also stands in stark contrast to the constant call given to every believer in the book of Revelation to overcome through following Jesus. So I suggest that at the root of this heresy is a spirit that perpetuates false divides and promotes all forms of false rulership over people. By suggesting this, I do not simply mean false divides of clergy/laity, but that in a first city it will work itself out in every context of the life of the city, with divisions on economic, racial, gender and every social distinction possible being propagated.

For success to come in a first city there has to be a hatred of all works that falsely divide. (In Pergamum there was a place given to the teaching of the Nicolaitans, but in Ephesus they had to even hate their works.) In a first city there has to be a calling for the voices from the margins. The voice of Jesus that comes through *"the sound of rushing waters"* has to be called for (Revelation 1:15). The central ground has to be occupied by Jesus, not by some super elite.

There is a controlling spirit that has to be confronted in first cities. That control spirit will seek to lock up initiative to the few, whereas the promise of Jesus is that He gives the right to all to eat of the tree of life in such a city (v. 7).

A key scripture for first cities is Isaiah 54 where the barren woman is told that she will bear children. A first city is a mother city – a place of birth. In order to break through there are some responses that have to be made, and one of the key areas is to "enlarge the site of the tent." In other words new ground has to be staked out. That new ground is staked out as the people of God move out into new areas of their city. This takes faith and risk on their part and it takes a leadership who are willing to permission people to move out. For birth to come, enlargement has to take place; for enlargement to take place there has to be a spirit of permissioning that is granted.

The third area of ensnarement (and the one that the Ephesian church was guilty of) is that of losing a first love for the Lord. A passionate heart desiring after His presence must fill the hearts of the believers in a first city. Those cities can begin so many new things, projects can be initiated, but passion must always take precedence over projects. Love for Jesus must be at a higher level even than that of amazing worthy deeds.

Any passion for Jesus has to outwork itself horizontally. Relationships therefore are key. Even time wasted with each other will never be wasted in a first city. This might be seen as a luxury in many eyes, but this sowing into relationships will cut right across the tendency of separating on the basis of doctrine or practice.

Two other factors in Ephesus

When Paul came to Ephesus there were two major earthly confrontations (see Acts 19). A confrontation with the heavenly power, as represented by Artemis of the Ephesians, resulted in a clash with the two powers that manifested on earth, represented by occultic and economic powers.

So, in impacting such a city it is vital that we do not shrink from encounters of this kind. First cities are places of significant bondage, and being birthing cities they attract some key occultic powers to themselves. There will have to be some heavenly warfare to see such a city come free. On the surface Masonic powers will be strong, but they are simply a modern manifestation of more ancient powers that seek to rob the Lord and His people of the city's gift. Alongside the Masonic will be hidden and overt centers for the occult. So warfare in heaven will bring the believers in a first city to come into contact with those who are committed to the occult (and I include the Masonic in that term).

A major key to seeing freedom come is also to recognize that the powers ruling over the economics of the city are strong. We are not to be afraid of wealth, but it is so vital that the believers in a first city do not sell out to the spirit of greed. There comes a point of time when the finances of such a city get unlocked to the Kingdom, but this normally only comes after a period of the church in the city being stretched financially, and often after having found that the city has been blocking any significant advance on such things as obtaining property in the city. Before there is a breakthrough, the city will seek to determine where and what the church can have within it.

When a breakthrough occurs, a major shift takes place with respect to these two powers. This will often mean that, where economic powers are wrongly tied up, there is an exposure of what has been wrong, and there can be an expectation of some who fall rapidly from power. It also means that, when the breakthrough comes, there is a new beginning and the church begins to receive favor, and sometimes from surprising quarters. In Acts 19, in the account of the riot that takes place in Ephesus, there is one intriguing verse that states:

"Even some of the officials of the province, friends of Paul, sent him a message begging him not to venture into the theater."
(Acts 19:31)

Paul had wanted to enter the theater to help quell the riot but this would have been a most dangerous situation for him. The disciples with Paul urged him not to do this, and then Luke records that *even* the officials took the same line. What makes this so remarkable is that it is these same officials, known as Asiarchs, who were the ones in power in the city and they were even the ones who made the appointments of those to position within the occultic Artemis cult. They were not disciples of the Lord, but were friends of Paul. Favor from surprising quarters!

Permission to eat

> *"To him who overcomes, I will give the right to eat from the tree of life, which is in the paradise of God."*   (Revelation 2:7)

What a great promise from Jesus to those who live within a first city. Although these promises are eschatological and will be fulfilled fully when Jesus returns, we are to manifest in the here and now what it will be like in the here (not "there," as Jesus is returning, rather than us "going") and then. So in a first city there has to be a tremendous freedom to go eat of this tree. What would that entail?

The tree of life is in contrast to the tree of knowledge of good and evil. That tree offered a short-cut way to being like God. In a first city we have to resist the temptation to make a name for ourselves through knowledge. It is by the grace of God, not through human achievement, that something will be established. In the Garden of Eden we read that the eyes of Adam and Eve were opened and they realized that they were naked. The vulnerability of nakedness was not the problem, and in eating of the tree of life there will be a vulnerability knowing that only God can cover us. There must be a resistance to having all the answers in a first city. All we are to know is that He is calling us to eat, and our experience of that is good. In a first city we do not know the end of the story but we are committed to beginning some new chapters.

In Luke's Gospel there are eight occasions when Jesus eats meals. The eighth (representing a new start) is with the two on the road to Emmaus (probably a husband and wife, thus paralleling Adam and Eve who took food and ate). When He gives them food and eats with them we read that *"their eyes were opened"* to see Jesus (Luke 24:31). In the Garden of Eden their eyes were opened to understand their own shame after eating of the tree of knowledge of good and evil, whereas once they eat of the tree of life true revelation follows.

Revelation does flow in a first city, but only in the risky environment of continual new beginnings.

Later in Revelation (22:2) we read that the tree of life is everywhere in the transformed city. Or, more specifically, the tree of life appears wherever the river of God flows. In a most enthralling book on Trinitarian theology (read it and you will never believe that theology has to be dull) C. Baxter Kruger throws out the challenge to find the river of God. He says:

> "What happens to the poor people who work the program, who do the Church thing, who follow the blind man in his bizarre religious ritual? Do they find the river, the dance, the glory? They are left sad and empty and bored and angry and depressed, and most seriously confused about Jesus. What happens to little boys and girls who know in the depth of their souls that there is a river of glory running through life and are told that this thing that the Church has invented is the river?
>
> The Western Church faces a new problem these days, the likes of which it has never faced. The problem for the Western Church today is that people have done what the Church told them to do, they have done what the preachers told them to do, they have followed the program, the bizarre religious ritual with its Bible labels. And they have found no glory, no river, no great dance."[2]

The river cannot be contained by our meetings, the river is to be found in our cities. If the tree of life is found wherever the river is, it is vital that in a first city the people are permissioned to take a risk and eat wherever the river is flowing. They must be allowed to go into the city, into all its spheres, and discover the fruit that grows when the people of God connect with the presence of God.

Only by so doing is there a hope of there being fruit in every month. "First" city and "safe" city do not go together. First and risk go together; first and freedom; first and fruit. Sounds dangerous? Well, the only safeguard has to be the passion for Jesus, not the passion for a project or even for a new way of doing church.

Mother cities are destined to bear fruit, and wherever the life of God is found there is such an abundance, we are told, that even the leaves provide healing for the nations. So, finally, in a first city we are going to expect a release of peace and reconciliation for nations. There will be many who come to a first city to study or to work, but who will meet their destiny. Many will discover that they came and were part of God's great mission field, but left with mission and healing in their hearts.

What about finishing what we start?

Not to start something really is a sin in a first city. Yet there is no great value in starting many things and finishing none. God wants what we start to be finished. One way in which things will be finished in a first city is to partner with other places and receive help from them. But there is one other element in a first city, and that is that there is a measure of latent gifting to finish. It is key, though, to know how to see that gift rise, and the key is to know that the gifting rises when the city has experienced failure. (By the way failure is not all it is cracked up to be – sin and never risking anything are far worse!)

Peter, the disciple of Jesus, is someone who could certainly be described as having a "first" gifting. He is always first to speak (and put his foot in it), first out of the boat to walk on the water, first to enter the tomb although he had been outrun by John. Peter assured Jesus that he was well aware of the weaknesses of others but that he would not fail him. How much he needed failure. Yet, it is in the light of his forthcoming failure that Jesus speaks to him that that after his denial of Jesus and when he has "turned back" that his role will then be to go and "strengthen" his brothers. I suggest that his turning back is in his passion for Jesus, but also in embracing His call, in spite of failure. Indeed, the grace of God is that through failure there will be a "strengthening" gift released. This strengthening gift is the grace to enable others to complete their course.

So, in a first city there is a latent finishing gift that is released after failure has occurred. A first city will have failures – and perhaps more than other cities. However, if they can continually be turned back in passion to the Lord, and be encouraged to embrace their gift for the sake of the gospel they will discover that they will increasingly begin to see what they have started finished.

We say then to the first cities in our nations: come on, you first cities. We need you to arise. You don't have to succumb to old unfruitful ways. You can persevere and hold to a passion for Jesus in the face of criticism. Press on and see all the dividing walls come down. Show us that there are always new beginnings in God. Come and tell us of the tree of life, come and partner with many who need your gifts. Come and be a first in our nations. Don't let failure put you off. Even if you fail we will call for you to rise again. We know that you will find levels of grace from heaven to persevere, and you will come to our aid to help strengthen us, too. We need your faith and we need your partnership.

Notes

1. I have used standard commentaries to research the historical background of the seven churches.
2. *The Great Dance* by C. Baxter Kruger. Perichoresis Press 2000 ISBN 0-9645465-4-X, p. 74.

Chapter 10

Smyrna: City of Deliverance

(Revelation 2:8–11)

Smyrna was some thirty-five miles north of Ephesus, renowned for its beauty and civic pride. It was a deep-water port, and the city competed with Ephesus over trade. Politically over the years Smyrna had made some very astute moves and was in excellent relationship to Rome. The city also had well-planned streets and a huge theater.

The reason for calling this a deliverance city is drawn from the clear oppression in which the believers find themselves. It is reminiscent of the bondage of Israel in Egypt. I believe God wants to bring deliverance in these places to demonstrate that He alone is the Savior and Deliverer. We might also have called this type of city a facilitating city, for in the purpose of God such cities are not intended to be in a place of rivalry with a first city (Ephesus) but to be in partnership, enabling what is birthed there to be further enhanced and facilitated.

Jesus comes to a deliverance city

Jesus is the *"First and the Last,"* the one who has *"died and came to life again"* (v. 8). Taking each phrase separately, it seems to me that the important element in the first phrase is that Jesus is "the Last." He not only begins a work but He finishes it. As with the Exodus God did not just send Moses with a message but with a corresponding anointing to persevere and finish the work of deliverance. Jesus, the First and the Last, certainly suffered oppression from the powers, and eventually He offered His life up, but that was not the end of the story. He was raised on the third day, never to die again.

Grasping hold of the Jesus who comes with this greeting is key for these cities, for the church will normally find itself suffering oppression in such places, and needs to receive the Jesus who has also been oppressed but is now alive with the title of being the "Last" as well as the one who begins all things.

It is vital that faith rises in these cities for a level of break-through that will result in stories being told of what the Lord has done in their city. For this faith to rise strong persistence will be required (and as we will read later, the church will often face even greater levels of oppression yet), so only a connection to the one who always finishes what He begins and who destroys death in His path will suffice.

Some central characteristics

Although the historical Smyrna was not a poor city, it is my experience that these deliverance-type cities frequently suffer from more oppression than other places, and oftentimes this oppression also has an economic dimension. It is not uncommon to find some measure of deeply embedded rivalry in their roots. So, for example, the city might have come into being, or gone through a period of significant growth, through the input of someone whose motivation was a vision of the place gaining a name of significance. This significance is often measured in direct comparison to somewhere else, so that a seed of rivalry is sown deep within. These cities are also often oppressed or exploited by a neighboring city.

Seeking to make a name for themselves is a characteristic of Smyrna-type cities. Smyrna was called "the pride of Asia," and a group of buildings on Mount Pagos was called "the crown of Smyrna." However, seeking to establish a name for oneself often flows from a sense of low self-esteem.

The fortunes of these cities seem to be able to swing enormously, and bearing in mind that they can manifest enormous economical differences I, somewhat tentatively, suggest that some of the central characteristics of these cities are as follows:

- A root, or significant manifestation, of rivalry. When the city is successful, then a level of pride will manifest; when not successful, the result will be of inferiority and shame.
- There will be a tendency to compare the city to elsewhere, and when the city becomes unsuccessful it can even become a place that is the object of humor.
- It will tend to exhibit oppression from within when successful, but it will be oppressed from without when there is perceived failure.
- It will exhibit both a strong predatory element and also a victim tendency. The predatory element will again manifest from within when the city is perceived to be prospering, but will come against the city from outside at other times. This predatory element will often manifest in the political arena. The victim element will be experienced in the lives of many of those who live within the city.

Surface strongholds

There are a number of aspects that immediately present themselves as evidence of a lack of breakthrough. If there are no fresh initiatives in the church, or when there are no initiatives that are being seen through to the end, we can be very certain that the city is not going to experience imminent breakthrough. Whenever the church is living from a spirit of insignificance, or motivated simply to demonstrate that it is a suitable rival to a church elsewhere, again we know that the spirit over the city is shaping the life of the church, not vice versa.

We can also be fairly confident that when only one expression of the church has developed in those cities to a place of prominence and when it is self-centered, no real breakthrough is taking place. This is one of the more sobering aspects, for in all honesty it is possible for such a church to be as much dependent on the spirit of rivalry and oppression as it is on the Spirit of God. So even when a largish church manifests in those cites, that can be most misleading. This might simply indicate that it has (unwittingly) come under the predator spirit and exploited the oppressed in order to make a name for itself. The church that will win through in a deliverance city will be a truly servant church that does not succumb to predatory ways.

Enemy strategies

In the letter itself we find that Jesus directly highlights some areas that the church is in danger of being locked up by, areas that are strongholds over the church. However, the very context of the church indicates one of the major strongholds that manifests here. The church is said to be under affliction. The Greek word *thlipsis* carries with it the sense of being squeezed or restricted, thus being put under extreme pressure. This is a good description of what takes place in this city-type. There is a twofold spirit at work over the city, either in the sense that there are two spirits at work or that there is one spirit manifesting in two ways. Let me for brevity's sake explain the scenario as if they are two spirits.

Without seeking to be exact in my terminology, I suggest that the two spirits that cooperate together over these cities are that of the predator and of the victim spirit. These two actually need one another for they feed off each other. For there to be a victim there has to be a predator, and the predator is always in need of a victim to prey on. Ironically they are both based in poverty: the victim spirit can clearly be understood as fostering poverty at every level, but the predator spirit, too, in seeking to take possession of what is not its by right is also based on a poverty mentality.

Hence, in these cities the discovery of where these two spirits are at work will be a major key in finding the means to bring the city through to freedom. The church will have to come in the opposite spirit to the dominant spirits over the city, and in due course we will explore what that would mean. (At this stage, though, it is important to underline that the church must not in any way succumb to the predator spirit.) As noted above, the very possibility that the church can grow (to a certain level) in these types of cities through exploiting the needs of those in the city, makes it vital that the church should be a servant seeking to facilitate true freedom. There can be a subtle twist on this where the church corporate takes a strong central position, and people have a sense of freedom through identifying with the success of the corporate Body. This is normally where there is a strong centralized leadership structure with honor and respect flowing one way (to the center) and truth flowing in the opposite direction. By fostering such a type of church it is possible to find some quick success, but this will not be effective in disempowering the actual spirits over the city. In fact, the irony of such a scenario is that the very powers themselves could be further empowered through the perceived "success" of that expression of church.

It is vital that the church in such a city truly becomes the servant of all with a strong empowerment of the Body being at the heart of what takes place. The gifting in the city is to set free and to facilitate. The story to be told is of God's deliverance of His people. So the church must not draw attention to itself as a corporate body but must place itself in such a way that it is among the people and there to serve.

Given that there is a strong poverty spirit in these cities, it will prove to be important that the church is reaching out to those who have found that circumstances have conspired to leave them poor. It is the disenfranchised that are always among those whom Jesus wishes to bless, and never is this truer than in these places.

(I will come back to these two issues of predator and poverty when we look at the keys to breaking through.)

Another aspect that affects the church in Smyrna is that of blasphemy (or slander) from those who claim to be something that they are not. (Like Philadelphia the church has to know that it is legitimate – as an accusation of illegitimacy is the central accusation that comes from "the synagogue of Satan.") Jesus promised His disciples that they would be spoken against, but it is important that the different church expressions speak well of each other. They are not to submit to a spirit of rivalry among themselves. They must reverse every curse through a constant flow of blessing.

When slandered by those outside the church, it is, however, the fear that can result from this affliction and slander that can become a stronghold over the city. This is particularly true when there is no promise from Jesus to change things round quickly. Indeed, to Smyrna, He promises that the circumstances that bring the pressures will even get worse, with some being thrown into prison. Perseverance that takes the church beyond the fear barrier is vital in these places, for breakthrough is not an overnight phenomenon.

Keys to breakthrough

There are three keys to breaking through that Jesus highlights. The first we find in Jesus' instruction to the church to see themselves as those who are rich; the second is found in His command that they are not to fear; and the third is implicit within the promise that they will not suffer the second death – they have to set right priorities.

Jesus makes no promise about immediate deliverance from affliction, but He commands the church to acknowledge that they are not in any way poor. The church has to break the victim mentality. The church has to become a deliverance church. Even if it seems as though they might have died, they are to so know that Jesus is the one who is risen from the dead (and the one who raises the dead) that their sense of richness increases.

First, then, the only way to break the victim spirit is to know that one is rich. But also the only way to refuse to succumb to the predator spirit is to know that one is rich. This means that the church is to be like a wedge standing between those two spirits. As the church takes this stand, inevitably the affliction becomes worse. Through choosing this position the church willingly takes on the pressure from both sides. Often in the process of discovering and declaring their richness in Christ the church will come under severe criticism from outside, and there will be ecclesiastical powers that will seek to exert an authority over it. The church in the city needs relationships outside the city, but they are also to know that they are not dependent on superior ecclesiastical knowledge based elsewhere for their breakthrough. Indeed, any help from outside has to be marked by a true servant spirit that does not seek to own but rather comes in to affirm the richness in the Smyrna-type city.

Second, Jesus instructs the church not to be afraid. Difficult days are ahead, but, as with Israel in Egypt, deliverance will come in due season. There are truly some wonderful stories to come from these places, and some of the early signs of breakthrough in a nation, I believe, will come in these types of cities. The pathway is not an easy one, though, and severe affliction (and even death) will often mark that pathway. Through suffering there will be the experience of deliverance.

Third, alongside the declaration of richness and the perseverance in the face of fear, there is the need to set long-term priorities. Jesus does not promise freedom from affliction, and indeed tells the Smryna church to be faithful even to death, but He does promise them freedom from the second death.

The church in the city must, therefore, set out priorities that are not based on short-term gains, but on long-term transformation. The eschatological crown of life will be experienced, in measure, in the city becoming what it was meant to be. A crown will be gained, not from proving itself as superior to elsewhere, but as the city comes right through to be one of the places that releases so much help to enable other places to break through.

The three keys to breakthrough seem, then, to be: receiving the affirmation of richness; not shrinking back from the task through fear; and the setting of long-term goals for transformation. These attitudes and actions may seem mundane, but they will connect with God's delivering power. The testimony will be one of God's deliverance not one of self-deliverance.

Smryna's gift released

From a superficial perspective the city might be doing well and prospering (and probably exhibiting a pride in its achievements), or it might be experiencing oppression, setbacks and living with shame, but either way, as the church stands in the gap, God will use it as an instrument to release the intrinsic gifts of the city.

Stories of God's deliverance will often begin here in these cities. That is why I believe God will frequently bring through something truly apostolic in these places – for it is a people who have come through affliction that He can trust will not abuse His authority.

These places will also find an effective partnership with first places (Ephesus-type cities). They will be supportive to and facilitate the initiatives that spring from there. And in partnership together with first cities they will form an efficient team that will enable establishing cities (Pergamum-type cities) to find their destiny.

They will bring a gift of facilitation as they work with other places. And given the facilitating nature of the city there will often be ministries released in those places that will be solely committed to facilitate others breaking through.

Another gift is the release of models of radical lifestyle as the true priority of spiritual richness is explored, and the desire to live in the light of the second death is embraced.

We so need these places to break through in our nations. To let us know that the Lord does not abandon the poor and the needy. So we say, come on all you deliverance cities and nations. We must hear your story, that though you were poor and oppressed, you found that in Christ you had all the richness that anyone could need. Come, break through and tell us that, though affliction can increase, there is a day of deliverance that comes. Come and partner with other places, show us how to serve and facilitate the dreams of others. Come and work with the places that are so sure they have everything, but are truly in danger of submitting to the authority of Satan's throne. We need you.

Chapter 11

Pergamum: the Establishing City

(Revelation 2:12–17)

This city was a place of great learning. Here was housed an enormous library which was second only to the library at Alexandria. The connection of Pergamum with literary activity was so close that the word "parchment" was derived from the name of the city. It was also a deeply religious place with the god Asklepios (the god of healing) being a major focus for worship. Medicine was also a feature of the city and the impressive medical school had a mile-long entrance lined with statues of body parts that had been healed.

Pergamum was a well-ordered city – being one of the first places to use city planning, with the top of the city being kept for public buildings, the next area for the wealthy, followed by the marketplace and then a district for the poorer residents beneath that.

Physical characteristics

Although a city has a spiritual life – and it has to be discerned according to the spiritual characteristics not the physical ones – there are often physical characteristics that show up in cities of different types. In these "establishing" cities some of the characteristics tend to be:

- They make space for education. Typically this will be seen with the presence of significant places of education, such as a university and diverse schools.

- Hospitals and, in particular, medical research will prosper in these cities.
- Typically they give attention in the planning aspect to how the city is laid out, and they seek to ensure that there are open spaces such as parks. These cities are normally very pleasant places to live.
- Access to and through these places is often very good.
- There is often a focus on the past.

Jesus comes to the establishing city

Jesus comes to Pergamum with the sharp two-edged sword. That sharp sword issues from His mouth and is destructive to everything that opposes Him. Of all the greetings this one is the most "violent." Jesus is very definitely in a warfare mood upon entry. This is an encouragement, for even if Satan has established a throne here (v. 13) we can be assured that Jesus will not make peace with the enemy. However, it is not only against Satan that He comes but also against those who are within the church but have compromised (v. 15).

His approach tells us that these cities cannot be allowed to rest back in passivity. They might be centers of learning and excellence, but that is not enough for they are called to press in to their inheritance. There is a certain amount of imagery in the letter drawn from the wanderings of the people of Israel in the wilderness, and the great challenge facing those people (and this city) was of fulfilling their call. It was possible to have provision from heaven while in the wilderness, but the true calling was not to stay there and give testimony to God's provision, but to establish a presence in the land itself, so that the land yielded its fruit for the people of God. So, in coming to the city, Jesus confronts the church, calling them to move on and enter into their redemptive purpose.

These cities can be extremely hard to work with but, when they break through, they bring testimony of the very definite advance of the Kingdom, with a good measure of signs and wonders.

Surface strongholds

As mentioned, the imagery for Pergamum is drawn from the wilderness and conquest periods of history. The purpose of leaving Egypt is to enter the land, and the challenge is of journeying right through the wilderness and refusing to stop off prematurely. In the wilderness God made provision for the journey with manna, but this type of provision was only ever meant to be temporary. It was the fruit of the land from which the people were to eat. It seems apparent, then, that the following immediate strongholds will manifest in these cities:

- Given the emphasis on education and learning, there will be a reliance on knowledge and traditions that have been passed on. There will be a tendency to reject anything new.
- Leadership will be non-confrontational at a relational level, but willing to teach publicly in such a way that others are put in their place. This is due to the teaching nature of the city, whereas Jesus comes with direct confrontation.
- Divisions that occur in the Body will often be based on doctrine. Correct teaching is given a higher value than committed relationships.
- Given the orderliness of the city, there will be a sense that the church knows where everything fits, but does not make room for the prophetic word of God. These cities are not good at handling prophetic ministry, wanting to qualify what has been brought to the point where it has all-but been disqualified. The message these cities send out to the prophets is that the church is doing well, so don't disturb it.

Enemy strategies

Given the nature of the gifting of such a place, it will be the surface strongholds that will become immediately manifest. If the calling is to press in to the land and therefore be a place of effective strategy and warfare, it becomes self-evident that the enemy will love to see the church simply wander in the wilderness with no forward momentum. There can be great starts in these places, but on closer examination all that takes place is history repeating itself. A new church or even movement can begin with great promise, but end up wandering while still believing its own publicity that it is cutting edge. Years later another church movement can begin in the same city only to repeat the cycle of history.

The deeper level strategies, though, can be seen through the discerning eyes of Jesus who releases His prophetic insight in this letter. It is to these central issues I now turn my attention. He highlights three aspects: that at Pergamum was located Satan's throne, and that there were two areas of teaching that were a problem. I will begin by looking at the two aspects of teaching.

Jesus draws attention to:

- those who hold to the teaching of Balaam
- and those who hold to the teaching of the Nicolaitans.

In Ephesus the church was commended for hating the *works* of the Nicolaitans but, given that Pergamum type-cities have a teaching orientation, it is appropriate that it is the teachings that are causing problems here. Although there will be a tendency for pride to grow over having correct doctrine, there can also be a tolerance that allows two issues to go unchallenged.

The first is that of compromise. Balaam was hired to curse the people of God but found that he could not curse what God had blessed. If that was all he had come against the people of Israel with, that might have been the end of the problem, but later we find that the real curse he introduced was the one of compromise. In Numbers 25 (and made clear in Numbers 31:16) we discover that he had been instrumental in leading the people into false relationships through advocating sexual relations with Moabite women. Even the leaders among the people had not stood their ground, but they too had compromised. It was only through the violent response of Phinehas that the people were spared.

So the enemy will allow leadership to be present in this type of city that will teach good clear doctrine, but will go for the soft option. There will need to rise up those like Phinehas with a passion for purity who will be instrumental in bringing about a breakthrough.

The class system seems to me to be at the heart of the Nicolaitan problem. So, the second of the two issues is control. Control will outwork itself in little room being given for fresh initiatives to spring up. What is in place will be seen as enough. This is why, I believe, in these places the new often comes to the city through youth. It is not uncommon for something to break out in and around (for example) a university campus. The impetuousness of youth becomes a tool in the hand of God to shake up the status quo. In the story of Israel the wilderness became the graveyard for a whole generation who left Egypt with the promises of God but did not finish their task, and it was a new generation that entered the land.

In partnership with the control issue is one of compromise. Passionate discipleship will mean that risks are taken. It will mean running the risk of being misunderstood. A low-risk leadership in these cities will never pattern the way to the breakthrough point.

The third central issue at Pergamum is the location of "Satan's throne" in the city. There is debate as to what this alluded to historically. Among the many possibilities that are suggested, the following three are the most likely "candidates:" it could have been a major altar to Zeus; or the judge's bench where the proconsul sat; or even the shape of the hill on which the city was built. The inability of scholars to decide on this issue leads me to believe that there might well be a more profound implication for us. Given that these cities are often pleasant places to live in, it is very easy to be fooled into believing the lie that everything is good and that problems are at a minimal level. The church then needs the very stark reminder that they battle not against flesh and blood but against principalities and powers in the heavenly realm. Perhaps Satan's throne is also present in other cities, but in a Pergamum-type city there needs to be a major reminder that he is present, and present in power.

It is most likely, though, that the text does mean that there is a specific presence of Satan's strategic rule that has been established in these places. Its influence will spread from its seat in the city over a wider area. Hence, we can expect to find a strong presence of occult, often hidden, and these cities can be discovered to be at the center of elaborate patterns and even "grid-systems" of the enemy's strategy.

In one such city in Scotland we discovered a pattern over the city of a hexagram that was pinned to one historical and natural site and to five graveyards that circled the city. All graveyards were set up within a few years of each other (during a time of church division) and the center point of the hexagram passed right through an artificial high place erected by the same person who was behind the establishing of the graveyards. (A pentagram is used in the occult to draw the powers of demons to a place, whereas the hexagram is used to hold them there.) It was no great surprise that the spirit of death is so prominent and even visible in the city.

In another city, this time in the USA, some time ago a pastor showed me the grid pattern over the city that converted Satanists had shown to him. These occultists had used this grid to position people on key points in the belief that they could hold back the church in its advance. This church has persevered, opened right up to the prophetic, invested in the youth, and as a result is seeing an amazing breakthrough in signs and wonders. In a recent short visit to the city I had four encounters that took me outside the church boundaries (I went to two restaurants, a coffee shop and a hotel): in all four places I was met by staff in those places that were from the church. This church is making a sound in the Spirit that it is possible to establish something in the land. Their success, though, has only come through a violent and persistent embracing of what the Lord is currently saying and doing.

For this city to break through

I suggest that, in order for an establishing city to break through, a major key (perhaps the major key) is for there to be courageous leadership that rises into place. By leadership I do not simply mean those who are the recognized pastors, but those who (even like Phinehas) have the passion of Christ in their hearts and are willing to risk it for Him. However, this courageous leadership has to be free from the spirit of control. No measure of legalism will bring about a breakthrough, only passion for Christ and His purposes.

There has to be a breaking with tradition. Room has to be made for the prophetic, particularly given that the city has a strong teaching orientation. Teachers and prophets don't make easy bedfellows, but it is that combination that I consider can release something truly apostolic. Acts 13 tells us that the apostolic ministries of Paul and Barnabas were released when the teachers and prophets at Antioch spent time together ministering to the Lord. The church in the city needs not only to receive prophets, but what they put in place has to be prophetic. A large part of that has to be the empowerment of youth. Pergamum has a focus on the past: the empowerment of youth shows that we have a focus on what is to come. It demonstrates that, regardless of how much of God's provision is currently being experienced, it is not what we are settling for.

These cities must develop a warfare anointing. Jesus comes in warfare mode, and they have to receive Him in such a way. The teaching anointing finds the issue of warfare difficult, as certain aspects of warfare are less "provable" than the exegesis of texts, yet warfare is part of what these cities are to develop.

The Israelites' journey through the wilderness was, in part, to prepare them for war. Entry to the land was by means of promise of God *and* through their participation in the warfare that God was initiating.

The calling over these cities to enter the land is high. They will not fulfill everything necessary for the whole Body of Christ; they will not discover a foolproof method of success; but they are called to demonstrate that it is possible to get something significant established in the land. They are to inform us that, in spite of giants in the land, there is fruit that can be enjoyed.

This all comes, though, at a cost, and part of the cost is of developing a warfare anointing.

A major side benefit of breakthrough, when it comes, is the discovery of a true well of healing. It was in the wilderness that God first revealed His nature as a healing God (Exodus 15:26). He had healed before, but it was at the waters at Marah that the revelation came of who He was with respect to healing. It came at the price of first discovering that the waters were bitter. A church that sets itself toward healing will break through, but it will only come through persistence, and often after experiencing some bitterness. This well will also be strongly contested, for the city of Pergamum had a focus on a false god of healing, thus indicating that the enemy wanted to steal part of the birthright of this city.

Finally, Jesus promises

There are two promises here to those who overcome. They will be given some hidden manna and will be given a white stone with a new name on it that only those who receive it will know.

In Scripture manna is called "bread from heaven" (Nehemiah 9:15; Psalm 105:40), and in the Septuagint "food of angels" (Psalm 78:25). What is clear is that hidden manna is supplied from heaven. There is the promise of a supply on the journey that will sustain those who pilgrim. Against all the odds God will feed the people and strengthen them because entry to the land is not an immediate experience. Elijah had this experience when twice he was encouraged by an angel to eat food supplied from heaven (1 Kings 19:1–10). The prophet was in the wilderness and in the light of eating was able to go for forty days and forty nights without further food. This is so obviously a parallel to the work of Christ, who went into the wilderness for forty days and nights after receiving an anointing from the Spirit of God under the approval of His Father.

Hidden manna, then, is strength from heaven; we might almost describe it as a "secret" supply to enable travel through the wilderness, to sustain the people while they engage in the warfare necessary on the works of darkness. The battle is intense, but there is miraculous provision for a successful outcome.

The significance of the white stone with the name on it is again much debated among scholars, but a good explanation has been suggested along the following lines. The natural stone of the area was black but, for inscriptions on buildings, slabs of white stone were specially transported there for carving. If that is the historical background, then the stone was shaped in such a way as to define the purpose of the building and to declare to whom, or for what, it was dedicated.

For the overcomers the promises would mean something along these lines: they would be supernaturally supplied with bread from heaven for their journey in and through the wilderness, where they were destined for warfare. This would give them strength to overcome even where Satan's throne was, thus releasing the knowledge that the land itself will yield a harvest. They will then, like Jesus, plunder the goods through deliverance and healing, as they have been effective in first binding the strong man. These overcomers would also become those shaped by God rather than by the locality. And through knowing who they were, it would be they who defined what was being built and they who would leave their mark on it, having decided whom the building was dedicated to. They truly would be those who established a beachhead in the midst of enemy territory. They would be those who turned the desert into a fruitful place.

So we say, to all establishing cities and establishing nations: rise up at this time. God will give you an incredible level of supply so that you can embark on what others would consider is a risky and courageous path. But you will be able to do what has not been done before. You will even be able to impact where Satan has placed a throne. You will show to the other cities that healing is not a past experience, nor even a rare experience. So, welcome the prophetic in your midst. Invest in your youth. Do not be critical of the new things that God initiates in your city. As you do so, you will be the ones who define your city; you will demonstrate that your city is not a place where the throne of

Satan is, but the place that is dedicated to the Lord. You will have to be strong and courageous. His word will have to remain in your mouth and in your heart. But the promise is that the Lord will establish you in all your ways; you will be prosperous and successful. We call you through and rejoice at your success.

Chapter 12

Thyatira: the Model City

(Revelation 2:18–28)

Of all the seven cities Thyatira was probably the least significant, certainly in terms of size. Pliny the Elder dismissed it with the phrase "Thyatira and other unimportant communities." Yet, due to the roads that passed through Thyatira it was actually a busy trading place.

Although not significant size-wise, I suggest that it is the city that comes nearest to being a model city. This type of cities, regardless of their size, is anything but insignificant, as working models are so important. Structurally, in the set of seven cities in Revelation, it stands in the middle of the list and draws its imagery from the kingly period in Israel. However, by using the term "model" it is important that we do not err the other way and assume it will demonstrate every aspect of the coming Kingdom. A model is not a blueprint and cannot be copied in every aspect. Indeed, a model can even be improved on, but there always remains the need for working models that can be looked at and learned from.

The most unique aspect of the city of Thyatira was its great diversity. To give just one example, there were more trade "guilds" in Thyatira than anywhere else in Asia. And it is this aspect of great diversity that is one of the central factors in a model city.

If, as I suggest, a model city draws up aspects of all the other cities into itself, then again it becomes clear that such a city will manifest a greater level of diversity than elsewhere. So, when we come to the church in such a city it is important that the church manifests significant diversity. Unity is vital, but a bland uniformity does not demonstrate Kingdom realities. A unity displayed amidst diversity is the key to breakthrough in these places, and one of the greatest challenges in a model city is for the diversity to develop in strength.

Some important notes on a model city

Diversity is the key word for the model city. This has so many implications that have to be noted as one seeks to help develop such places. I list a number of them below:

- Since a model city draws up into itself elements from all the other cities, the potential strongholds that can manifest in a model city will also be diverse. It will therefore be harder to list out the typical strongholds of a model city. They could indeed vary from one model city to another.
- The central stronghold mentioned (that of Jezebel) will also manifest itself in the other cities. It is not unique here but can always find a concentrated expression in these places.
- The promise to rule is a promise to all the churches in every city. That is the destiny of the people of God, and ultimately the rulership of the earth is not simply for the believers in the model city, but for all believers in all cities. But here in a model city that rulership will be expressed as a picture of the whole, and for this reason the DNA of rulership will have to be right. It will have to be Christ-like and in these places it will also have to be diverse. The ruling is not simply in relation to the church, but the nations. Hence, any idea of a "city eldership" in these places would have to include those whose setting is also in the spheres of the city.

Jesus comes to a model city

Jesus comes as the "Son of God" (v. 18). Although a normal way by which believers describe Christ, here it is unusual in that this is the only reference to Jesus as the Son of God in the whole of Revelation. It stands in direct contrast to the local cultic worship of Apollo Tyrimnos (the sun god and son of the supreme god Zeus) and the claims of the emperor to be an incarnation of the gods. In a place where there were false claimants to the throne Jesus asserts His presence and claim. Moreover, Apollo was the god of prophecy, and here in Thyatira where there is the manifestation of false prophecy (through Jezebel's presence), Jesus is indicating that He comes with searching truth. We see this further with the description of Jesus as the one who has eyes *"like blazing fire"* and feet *"like burnished bronze"* (v. 18). There is a very definite presence of Jesus coming to the city, and that presence will be one of glorious holiness. He is the one who purifies because He hates sin. This is not a Jesus that one would mess with!

So, in this type of city we can expect there to be some sharp judgements on sin. There can be no room for tolerating compromise; there can be no rivals to Jesus. The city and church will manifest diversity, but the unifying factor will be Jesus' presence that lays all things bare.

Jesus comes with piercing sight, and this sight connects the model city with the cities that help initiate new things through their prophetic sight, and He comes with His feet ready to be planted, which connects the model city with those cities that establish a presence in the land and in creation.

Some central characteristics

Model cities will themselves be very diverse, so it is less easy to describe their central characteristics. They will differ from each other both in terms of their size and their history. The common element that they will share, however, is their internal diversity. This will likely be represented in some of the following ways:

- a great spread of nationalities and cultures
- the cuisine will be diverse, often with restaurants that offer food from cultures from around the world

- numerous religious affiliations
- a larger spectrum of church denominations and styles than might be expected in a place
- a variety of trades
- a model city will have within it model projects, and be conducive for the release of pilot projects
- a number of headquarters will normally be located in the city
- a number of model cities will indeed be regional (and perhaps even national) capitals
- many model cities will export something that might even go round the globe – Thyatira was famous for its purple dye (Acts 16:14).

Surface strongholds

The immediate strongholds that will manifest in these cities when they are not breaking through will be related to the diversity issue. Either the diverse expressions of the Body of Christ will not be held together in the bond of unity, resulting in widespread division, or the diversity that should be manifest in the city will not be expressed due to the strongest voice silencing all other voices. So, the immediate stronghold will either be that of division or of uniformity. The division will often be fed by the attitudes of a dominant leader, or church. The issue of unity is so important in these cities, for that is the basis by which the diversity can be fruitfully held together.

The possibility of abusive rulership is always close to the surface in these cities. The promise is to *"rule over the nations,"* and although it is true that Jesus shatters the nations like a piece of pottery, His authority was gained through laying down His life for them (vv. 27–28).

Enemy strategies

We can almost sum this up in one word: "Jezebel." The only proviso that has to be put in place alongside this comment is that the strongholds that manifest in the other six city-types can also manifest themselves here in the model city.

It is not likely that Jezebel is to be identified as a specific person, but the use of the name indicates the presence of a major stronghold. The marriage of Ahab to Jezebel was for political expediency, but opened the door to a major attack on the purity of devotion to Yahweh among the people of God and then to an open attack on the kingship in the land (see 1 Kings 16:30–32).

There was a toleration of this stronghold that is in such stark contrast to the Jesus who comes to Thyatira with a burning passion for purity. However, it cannot be tolerated, for the elements that are highlighted here are so destructive of the work of God.

The Jezebelic spirit will manifest itself in self-appointment, for we read, "she calls herself" a prophetess. Self-appointment is always a big giveaway. True servants of God carry a humility knowing that only God can appoint. The self-appointed nature of this spirit means that there will be significant opposition to what God has truly appointed – there will be an opposition to those that God has anointed to bring a godly lead.

There will be false claims made in the name of prophecy, which will be particularly focused against what is truly prophetic. In Elijah's day there had to be a showdown between the prophets of Baal and himself. The true prophetic voice had been silenced and not welcomed in the land. This false prophetic claim will often be outworked through teaching, for we read that Jezebel was "teaching" (v. 20).

We are told that Jezebel, through her teaching, was seducing the servants of God. The element of persuasion and relationship used is often very visible, for the word used here (in NIV translated "misleads") means more specifically to seduce through leading into error. There has, therefore, to be a bringing to the light of what the Lord has spoken and what He has promised, so that sin is exposed and everyone is held account-able to the word and promises of God.

Naboth is a good example of what the spirit of Jezebel seeks to do to the servants of God (1 Kings 21). Ahab had desired to have

Naboth's vineyard to turn it into a vegetable garden. The vineyard speaks of Naboth's place of fruitfulness in God and, although he refuses to give it up, Jezebel comes and joins herself to Ahab who abuses his position of rulership. Her challenge to him can be paraphrased, "Do you not govern Israel?" (1 Kings 21:7). There is, therefore, strong attack against the servants of the Lord and it can come through a wrong allegiance of those in leadership. In other words, this manipulating spirit is not simply a spirit that can work against leadership, but leadership can even be aligned to it and allow for people to be disinherited. Control, manipulation and even domination (the elements of witchcraft) can be exercised by people over leaders, and by leaders over people. Control is, indeed, just that – it is *over* people. We are not to have control over anyone, for Jesus died in order to preserve our freedom from control. When a Jezebelic spirit is strong, false accusation is also part of what manifests (1 Kings 21:10).

The seduction involves elements of compromise (eating food sacrificed to idols) and sexual immorality. The eating of the food sacrificed to idols in Thyatira was almost certainly tied to the many guilds, and the compromise was in order to make commercial gain. So there is a strong warning here about compromising with the city in order to gain financially. In the Old Testament sexual immorality is strongly linked to false worship, so its mention here is not necessarily a direct literal reference to sexual immorality, although where there are allegiances given to other people, and where there is a toleration of control, sexual immorality often follows.

Family life and true order are very much the object of attack. Indeed all forms of healthy relationships come under major attack when this stronghold is present, with confusion and suspicion often undermining straightforward relationships. When the spirit of Jezebel is strong, there is a perversion of the judgement that Jesus speaks. He says that He will judge her with sickness and that her children will experience death (vv. 21–23). The perversion that takes place is of sickness coming against everyone who seeks to pattern the work of God in these places and with a strong focus of attack on their physical and spiritual children.

Jesus exposes all that has gone on as being the *"deep things of Satan"* (v. 24 NRSV). Thyatira-type places can easily draw from other places and so be open to change, but they must always bring everything under the scrutiny of Jesus. They cannot be overly impressed and make a quick response, otherwise that which is embraced might prove to be totally destructive.

Breaking through

The Thyatiran church is told to *"hold fast to what you have"* (v. 25 NRSV). There has to be a strong contention here not to move away from what God has done. The temptation will be to let go, but the judgement of Jesus is very strong in this city. Unity is not a luxury, it is a necessity. Diversity is not an enemy, it is a necessity. Holding those two together is a wonderful challenge that requires true humility and honor from one part of the Body to the other. Diversity will have to be honored, and the church will have to work hard to maintain the right of diverse expression for one another.

Thyatira was also a first line of defense against any invading army. It was a little frontier city, and, spiritually, model cities are to be first-line-of-defense places. There are works of the enemy that can be stopped in their tracks there, and also ground can be gained there that can make for strategic advance into Sardis-type places.

As I write these paragraphs, I am in a city in California. Last night I prophesied concerning two cities in California, one of which is the city I am currently in and which today I understand is a Thyatira-type place. The other one I referred to is a definite and very classic Sardis-type city. I did not understand this element of "first line of defense" places last night but now can understand the prophetic word in the light of that. (To protect the identity of the places I will use Thyatira and Sardis in what I quote.)

I spoke these words: "Sardis is the big jewel to be gained, she

carries the same gifting as the state, but the keys to her release lie
in Thyatira. The strongholds manifest themselves in Sardis but
their roots are here in Thyatira. There has to be a bringing of this
city into line in order to release Sardis."

The promise through the model city

There are two promises. The first, in simple terms, is the promise
of rulership. Our idea of what it means to rule has to be
submitted to the rule that Jesus models. His is truly a servant
rulership. In the words of the song by Graham Kendrick He is
"the Servant King." This promise is not about lording it over, but
of establishing true order and rulership throughout the earth.
The authority is immense and (undeniably) spiritually violent,
but it flows from a place of humility and submission. The
authority Jesus gives is one that has been given to Him by His
Father. There is an order to this authority: the overcomers have
authority because they are under authority. Unless they exercise
their authority in a Jesus-like way they will fail to see their city
impacted.

The authority is an authority over that which stands against
the people of God and their advance. The rod of iron is almost
certainly the shepherd's club used for killing animals that
endangered the sheep. In ancient cultures it was not uncommon
to inscribe the names of the king's enemies on earthen pots
before ritually smashing them to symbolize the destruction of
the king's enemies.

So we can conclude that, as the church in the model city
preserves what God has given, and in humility submits to the
true king, an authority is released that is truly a delivering
authority to subdue the enemies of God. Hence, there are
strongholds that can be broken here that will have an impact
beyond the immediate geographical boundaries.

The second promise is that they will be given the "morning
star" (v. 28). As with many of the symbols it is not easy to be
definitive about the meaning. Since the morning star was viewed
in the ancient world as heralding the birth of a new day, it could

well be symbolic of life and light coming. Jesus Himself is described as the "morning star" in Revelation 22:16 which draws from Balaam's oracle in Numbers 24:17. There the emphasis is of a ruler arising who will crush the enemies of God. So, in all likelihood, the promise is another way of saying that there will be an impartation of authority from Jesus who has truly established God's Kingdom, through destroying every enemy. Perhaps the added element in this promise is that they will be aware (and see ahead of others) that the new day of God's presence is being heralded.

Final comments

Thyatira is placed between two sets of three cities. Pergamum ended that first set of three with the mandate to establish something significant in the land. Sardis follows on from Thyatira and begins a new set of three cities. With these next three God intends that there is an expansion of what has gone before. However, they are unlikely to be too successful without the model city taking the ground apportioned to it. And although the model city draws from all other cities, it is also key in helping release the Sardis-type cities that follow.

We call the model cities to rise. We call them to show us how the Kingdom of God grows through crushing His enemies before Him. We call them to maintain, and even rejoice in, their diversity. Show us how to be united under one Lord. Be the first line of defense when the enemy seeks to advance. Push back the enemy from the land that he has occupied. Come and open up space for cities of mercy to arise. Don't sell out to commercialism; stay true to what you have and you can cleanse so much in the nations. Don't submit to false prophecy but foster the Elijah anointing that will lead the way in bringing in the rule of Messiah.

Chapter 13

Sardis: the City of Mercy

(Revelation 3:1–6)

One of the first things we note on reading the letter to Sardis is how similar the risen Lord's greeting is to the one He brought to Ephesus. Both these cities are intended to be places of birth and beginnings, to initiate on behalf of others. Ephesus began a series of three cities and Sardis likewise begins a second series of three.

Sardis was a wealthy city with the gold-bearing river, the Pactolus, running through it making a significant contribution to its wealth. In Sardis we have the beginning of money in the modern sense of the word, with the first ever coinage in Asia Minor being minted here.

Sardis also claimed to have invented the process for dyeing wool and had been a major fashion center. Alongside fashion there was jewelry making and the city was also known for its music. Given the list of characteristics mentioned above, it is easy to see that Sardis was then a trend-setting city with a significant influence beyond its own immediate area. With arts, fashion and also its wealth this city was a "happening" place. Creative gifts were honored and flourished in this city.

Religiously the city honored the Anatolian goddess Cybele, and it was through the worship of this goddess of nature and fertility that another characteristic of the city developed. The worship was a wild frenzied affair with very few moral boundaries. Even on the lips of pagans Sardis was a name of contempt.

Its people were notoriously loose living, being both pleasure- and luxury-loving.

This last aspect means that the city was a place of great tolerance and here, as in so many cities of mercy, a level of acceptance and mercy toward people was exhibited. Mercy, that is, without judgement. This is not true mercy, for although mercy triumphs over judgement it does not eliminate it.

The characteristic mix in these cities means they are very open to a New Age-type invasion and will also allow all sorts of sexual practices to be accepted as a norm. (However, as per everything the enemy does, he can only pervert what is there. He does not come with an original creativity, but induces people to abuse the intrinsic characteristics of the place.)

In seeking to define the nature of this city we can call it a city of mercy, but also, given that it begins another set of three cities, we will discover that it can also be described as a city of development. These cities have a gifting which enables them to take what is happening and bring significant development to it.

Jesus comes to the city of mercy

As mentioned already, the greeting is similar to the one that Jesus brought to Ephesus. Both cities have the ability to birth new things for the sake of other places: Ephesus carries the true spirit of initiation, whereas Sardis brings the dimension of expansion and novelty. To both places Jesus comes with a universal aspect. In Ephesus He comes with the seven stars and walks among the seven lampstands; here in Sardis He comes with the seven stars and the seven spirits of God. The seven stars indicate that there is a destiny for the church as a whole that is being worked out in these places. These types of cities need to hold a strong faith that Jesus is building the church, that the gates of hell will not prevail against His work. So, the Sardis-type cities, like the Ephesus-type, must have a strong prophetic element to them particularly with respect to the destiny of the church. The unique prophetic contribution in the Sardis-type cities will be the ability to communicate the mercy of God and to encourage the church to think outside the box.

Jesus not only comes to Sardis with the seven stars, but also with the *"seven spirits of God"* (v. 1). I consider that this is easiest understood as a description for the fullness of the Spirit of God.[1] This surely must indicate that, if ever there were places that should manifest a fully orbed life of the Spirit of God, it should be these. A fullness of the Spirit will include a charismatic element but that will not exhaust His work. The fullness of the Spirit will mean that these places should resonate with the creativity of God, so the arts will flourish here. It will not be possible to establish an effective church in these places that is a boring expression of church. It will be vital that creativity is at the heart of any church that is going to break through. The fullness of the Spirit will mean that the people of God as a whole will be empowered, and not simply some elite leadership. These places of mercy carry a destiny to see a people movement released.

Surface strongholds

Following our pattern that we are using, some of the immediate strongholds that will manifest in these places of mercy are now evident:

- a stranglehold over creative gifts
- a tendency for one expression of church to claim to have the Spirit, thereby writing off other expressions of the Body of Christ
- a lack of any new developments or trends
- a controlling over-centralized style of leadership that seems to have a greater claim to having the Spirit of God than the Body; and often alongside that stronghold, ironically
- a teaching on grace that ignores the need for godly discipline, so releasing a tolerance without discernment.

All of the above are surface strongholds. If those elements are being manifested, we know that the church is not really breaking through to the place of harnessing the gifts of the city. There are, however, strategies of the enemy that we will need to understand in order to help the church bring the city to a place of openness.

Enemy strategies

Sardis, Jesus said, had a name for being alive – it had a reputation, but this was no longer a current reality. Past accomplishments and victories are wonderful as it is vital for every community to have stories of God's grace that can be recounted to subsequent generations. The danger, though, in the city of mercy is of only having past stories, rather than living testimonies. Sardis is rebuked for having a reputation for being alive. Having a reputation can be a deception. In Sardis there is no excuse for living off the past, for it is here that Jesus comes with the seven spirits of God.

There is also an inability to complete what has been begun, for Jesus says that their works have not been found perfect (or completed). Like the city itself, which had a great temple in honor of Artemis that was never completed, the church here had not brought to completion what they had started. Perseverance has to be developed in these places.

These two strongholds are related, for an over-focus on the past will mean that insufficient energies are given to the current task. This type of city is called to focus on the next phase of what God wants to release. There has to be a currency about these places; indeed, when these places are healthy there should be something like a restlessness in the people of God as they continually press in for something new. Bringing pastoral leadership to such situations is a challenge, but what cannot be accepted is where the church settles down and becomes passive.

Passivity or sleepiness is a third major issue highlighted in this letter to Sardis. The fortress part of the city was built on what was supposed to be an unassailable cliff, yet twice in its history the city was taken by surprise at night. Hence, a significant stronghold is that of passivity due to a false sense of security.

The three strategies of the enemy, then, that are highlighted in this letter are:

- a dependence on a past reputation
- a lacking of energy and focus toward developing new "trends"
- a passivity through a false sense of security.

The redemptive giftings

We can now put together the contribution that the Sardis-type of cities can make to the work of God in a nation. As cities of mercy they can become places that help everyone find their destiny and sense of belonging. Even when people have felt that they have not fitted elsewhere, they can flourish in these situations where they do more than simply find their place – they can also develop in their calling and significance. This will be particularly true for those who are creative and those who have gifts of innovation.

The sevenfold dimension of the presence of the Spirit of God in these places means that there can be wells of prayer and the prophetic open here for whole areas or even nations. They can become significant refreshing places for many people to come to, with copious amounts of the Holy Spirit being there to be drunk from.

As trend-setting cities the gifting that is released is not only to hear and see what God is doing but also to be willing to do things in ways that have not been thought of before. They have the ability to break patterns, not being hemmed in by previously developed structures, and that ability is so essential if the church is to break out to a new level. This, perhaps more than any other aspect, is the gift of these places.

In one such city in the UK where I have traveled, it is clear that room has been made for a great expression of the Holy Spirit. They have sought to honor the past, but not to live under a past reputation, and while they have continued to honor what has been, they are committed to open up a prophetic well in their area. One of the leaders sent me some papers on the future shape of the church and, when I read them, I was most excited. Excited, not because they contained a foolproof design for church, but because they were the first papers I had ever read where there was a plan not only for change, but also for non-existence of what was here already. In other words, the commitment to a new shape meant a plan to bring to an end what was already in place. It is easy for people to use such words as "we are open to changing our structures" but it is (sadly) rare for them to develop a strategy that will leave the present leadership disempowered and the Body empowered to do the works of service, and that will so release a new shape of church that the present shape will not survive. When I read the papers I was more than willing to make a commitment to those people.

Another aspect to these cities is that they are night cities. Jesus says in this letter that He will come as a thief at night. This aspect means that many of these places will have to develop prayer gatherings that begin to take back the night hours. "Watch and pray" will be a significant part of their task.

I spent a few days in Paris (a Sardis-type city) at the end of 2002 and, while there, was asking the Lord for revelation concerning the city. I was even speaking to the city, calling for her to reveal her characteristics. I felt as if I saw very little for some two days, but in the middle of the final night there, around 2.40 a.m., I was awoken and it was as if the city was present in the room. It came alive and there was revelation at night. Over the next two hours I had encounters with the Lord in the room as He showed me certain aspects of the city. The most significant was when I was taken in a vision to the bottom of the Eiffel Tower (I had never actually been there physically, and I consider it was a vision, although it was possibly something stronger than that). In that experience the Lord was speaking to me as He showed me how so many people come to the city and view it through romantic eyes. To come to Paris to propose marriage or to celebrate togetherness is a good thing in itself, but I began to weep as I heard the city saying, "Who will come here and make commitment to me?

Who will love me for who I am? Who will love me enough to commit themselves to me?"

A central issue in these places is to find those who will come and pay the price of loving the city for its own sake, rather than simply viewing it romantically. These cities can be romantic places to visit and even to live in, but they require a commitment, even to the level of covenant, in order to turn them around. Challenging, indeed, but I believe incredibly rewarding.

It was when I found out that the city revealed itself at night that I realized this was a Sardis-type of city, and my later discovery that Sardis had been a fashion center, was further confirmation (and, indeed, the gifting of the nation of France as a whole).

In line with the night element these places will also be very conducive to revelation coming to people in dreams. In Scripture dreams are a very common way by which the Lord reveals Himself or the future, and it is time that these hours are taken back. It is not uncommon to find believers being disturbed, particularly during occultic seasons, between 2.30 and 3.30 a.m., when the occultic curses come to a focus. We must proclaim that the night hours do not belong to the occult, and in Sardis-type cities it will become increasingly important to take them back.

A remnant will be enough

When Jesus speaks hope to Sardis, it is on the basis that there are those who *"have not soiled their clothes"* (v. 4). Jesus does not call for the many to turn the situation, but calls for the few. He wants to work with the few in order to turn the many. Numbers are not the key, but the cleanliness of the clothing worn by the few. There is probably another element beyond cleanliness that is indicated by the mention of wearing white clothing for, in the Roman world, citizens were often given white clothing to wear in order to celebrate a military victory. In Sardis' history the city had been captured twice as a result of not being alert at night. Now, by way of contrast, Jesus promises to give to those who are awake and watchful robes celebrating victory.

Alongside the white robes there are two other promises for the church in Sardis. First, their names will not be erased from the book of life. In both Jewish and Hellenistic cultures the erasure of a name meant exclusion from the community. (In Greek culture the names of those who committed a serious crime were erased from the civic register, and in the Old Testament removal of a name was associated with capital punishment.) And, second, their names will be confessed before the Father and the angels.

The word "name" occurs four times in this letter (v. 1, as a criticism of having *"a name for being alive"* (NRSV; v. 4, the few "people" whose clothes have not been soiled is literally a few "names"; and here in v. 5 where there are two references). In Scripture a person's name is an expression of his or her identity and the means by which authority is released. So, as with the other letters, the promise is eschatological and will be finally fulfilled at the *parousia*, but what will be true then has to be manifest now, so the key element for Sardis-type places is the promise that they will have an identity that is permanent and a level of heavenly authority (indicated by the confession of their names in heaven). This heavenly authority is contingent on dealing with any compromise that comes through fear, for in the Gospels we read that Jesus will, indeed, confess the disciples before God and the angels provided they are willing to suffer (Matthew 10:26–33; Luke 12:4–9). For the promises to manifest, there has to be a willingness to embrace whatever persecution is necessary.

Given this use of the word "name" in this letter, it becomes evident that those who want to engage in turning a Sardis-type place around will have to know who they are. Jesus does not work with the many, or simply with the few, but He works with the few "names." The "names" are those who know who they are and have a clear sense of their own identity. These ones are absolutely key in these situations. Such people then have to know that they have rights of inheritance (names written in the book of life) and that as a result their names are confessed in heaven. The promises for those who will commit themselves to these places are awesome. Angels can know the names of these people, and so again an expectation of angelic activity would be part of the gifting of these places.

Final comments

Given that the church is told to *"strengthen what remains"* (v. 2) and to *"remember what you received and heard"* (v. 3), there is a strong exhortation to make sure that they lay hold of what has already been deposited. A good Old Testament narrative for this is the re-digging of the wells by Isaac that his father Abraham had dug in a previous generation (Genesis 26:12–33). Twice he had to dig and contend with the Philistines over the wells that were re-opened, but then came the breakthrough as he opened up the well-named Rehoboth (meaning broad or roomy place). Given that the Sardis-type cities are developing cities, they have to make room for expansion and, in order to do so, they have to press through the contention and opposition.

The contention, though, is to enable the digging of a well of plenty. They are called to open up wells that have not yet been opened, to demonstrate that in spite of opposition there is more water than was previously thought. A significant sign of a turn-around in these places is when spiritually (and often symbolically) there is the breaking through to space and room to exist and to grow. Spiritually there comes the "feel" of freedom to breathe and the lack of oppression; symbolically it will often be marked by the release of new property, or some-thing similar, for the Body of Christ.

This establishing of the Rehoboth is to lead to the opening up of the well of covenant or sevens ("Beersheba"). Sardis-type places are eventually to demonstrate that even the enemies will have to acknowledge the favor of God that is on the Body of Christ. These places truly are developing cities, cities that do not stand still, that do not simply repeat what has gone on before, but demonstrate that boundaries can be broken. They become great partners for the gateway cities (Philadelphia: the subject of the following chapter). They are gifted to enable gateway cities truly to come into their own.

So we call you wonderful cities of mercy to arise. You have such a well to tap into, and we want to encourage you to do things that have not been done before. Be unashamed at developing what has been done elsewhere, and show that it can be taken to new dimensions. You can open up the rich wells of creativity; you can release dreams and dreamers. We need you so much. Our God has never been boring, so come show us this God who is alive.

Note

1. Some commentators have suggested that these seven spirits are seven angels, but given (1) that the stars are the angels and these are mentioned separately in this greeting, and (2) that the first mention of the seven spirits of God in Revelation comes in a greeting that seems to be Trinitarian (1:4–5), it is best to take this as a numeric way of communicating the fullness of the Holy Spirit.

Chapter 14

Philadelphia: the Gateway City

(Revelation 3:7–13)

Philadelphia was situated on the eastern edge of the Roman Empire, lying on the main trade route from Smyrna and also on the major Roman postal road from Troas to Pergamum. It was ideally placed for commerce and was called "the gateway to the East." Philadelphia was expected to introduce the Greek and Roman ways to the peoples of the East, so we can call it a "missionary city." The predominant imagery used in the letter is of a door or gate being opened in order that there could be free flow out from the city: hence, the terminology of Philadelphia being a "gateway" city.

Jesus comes to the gateway city

Jesus comes as the holy one, the true one. This sets the city in line with its purpose, for as the holy one (a title often used for God in the Old Testament, indicating His wholly otherness) Jesus is coming to them from another dimension, so that they will bring His presence into the dimension where they live. Like the city, which was to bring the presence of the empire into new territory, the church was to be impacted by the dimension of heaven in such a way that they become the gateway for heaven to the earth. As the true one, the church is to experience Christ as the one who is the benchmark for everything else.

When Jesus comes, He comes as the one with *"the key of*

179

David" with the authority to open and shut (v. 7). This is a clear reference to Isaiah 22:22 where there was a shift of authority from Shebna to Eliakim. Within the context of the Issaianic passage this spoke of access to the king and his palace. (There is also probably an allusion to Revelation 1:18 where Jesus states that He has taken the keys of death and Hades.) So, drawing these insights together, we understand that He is coming as the one who has taken authority and by inference the one who is giving the key to the church, so that they might exercise authority. The church is to know Jesus as the Gatekeeper and, therefore, to understand that they are the ones through whom He wishes to establish true authority.

Surface strongholds

There will be some immediate signs that a gateway place is not breaking through to its destiny. These can be easily understood as the locking up of the calling of the place. The gates in a gateway place are obviously very important. The place is called to be a place of connection and to release the presence of Jesus and the message of the gospel. So, when isolation marks the church, we know that no real breakthrough is taking place. The church in a gateway city is to make connections. These connections need to be first with heaven for, if gates are going to open, the first gate that must open is the one between heaven and earth.

It is the presence of a heavenly dynamic that must mark the church. There should be openness between heaven and earth, such as Jacob experienced at Bethel (Genesis 28:10–22). There he experienced in a dream angels descending and ascending and understood that the place was a gateway from heaven to earth. These places should give good access for the inbreaking of the supernatural, which will include the receiving of dreams.

Jesus' coming as the holy and true one leads us to understand that, if there is a twisting of truth in these places, then there is no real breakthrough occurring. This twisting can be in terms of morality or doctrine, but when cults abound and the church is in a place of compromise, then the gateway city is to be considered bound.

A very significant marker in gateway cities is the issue of who the gatekeepers are. The quote concerning the "key of David" from Isaiah is all to do with a change in the gatekeeper. When the church is not impacting these cities, there is a very strong opening for the wrong gatekeepers to take positions of authority. A major sign of shift in the spiritual atmosphere is when there is a change in the "guard," with the result that those who occupy positions of leadership become favorable to the righteous rule of God. When the church begins to occupy her rightful place, then the gates become open to those who will serve.

Enemy strategies

There seem to be three main enemy strategies that Jesus exposes over the city. The first is that of a spirit of blindness. Three times in the course of two verses (3:8–9) Jesus says, "behold" or "see" (the command form of the verb *horao*, to see is used, although most English versions do not translate this word each time). Given the threefold emphasis in these two verses we can see how vital sight is in these places. They are destined for sight and the enemy will both seek to bring about blindness in the church and also to steal the gift of sight for others to exploit wrongly.

Indeed, given that Jesus immediately commands the church to see, we can understand that the breakthrough in the city will begin with sight and will only be sustained through sight. If there is no sight, then there will be no breakthrough. Jesus says the church has but little power, but it is vital that the church does not believe that an increase of power is the answer. Rather, it is an increase of sight that will release the power, and not vice versa.

A gateway city should have more sight than it feels comfortable with. The vision must be beyond its ability to fulfill, and the sight that is restored is not just for the immediate city. I was in a gateway city in Wales back in 1999, before I ever understood the different nature of cities, but began to prophesy that in this city it was possible to see the whole of Wales, saying that "in a gateway city it is possible to see a whole region or even a whole nation." I now understand that this is the case. If one wants to see what is outside an area one has to go to the gate or the door. So, the sight to be recovered in these cities will be sight for the region, and this is why the enemy will work overtime in shutting down this gift.

Not only will there be a shutting down of the gift, but the nature of the spiritual realm is such that, when there is a failure by the people of God to take up the gifting of an area, it is there for some alien spiritual power to pick up. Oftentimes these places will have a significant historic presence of Freemasonry with its use of the "all-seeing eye." Given that Freemasons also use a blindfold (known as a "hoodwink") in their initiation rites with the confession that the initiate is in need of sight through the light of Masonry, it is easy to see how there is space for them to gain a significant position in the city if the church does not press in for the sight that the Lord intends.

The geographic setting of the meeting places of such cultic groups as the Mormons and Freemasons is often fairly central, but as the city develops there is often the drawing to the gates (the literal physical entry points). (Joseph Smith, the founder of Mormonism, was a disgraced Mason and many of their rites simply parallel those of Masonry.) In mapping such cities it is certainly a good practice to examine any old gates/entry points to the city as well as new ones to see what has been established in them.

In one city I have visited in California there is an imposing Masonic Temple in the center of the town, while on the south "gate" a large Mormon Temple has been erected. Between the two is an archway proclaiming (rightly) that the town is a gateway, but when I was in a neighboring town I had a dream of this archway being erected with some form of sacrifice. (This could mean that the arch was erected on an old sacrificial site, or perhaps it was erected with Masonic rites or through something like a Masonic connection.) I suggest that the town was being claimed as a gateway into the region for wrong spiritual powers.

While I was in that region in 2003, the church in the gateway town prayer-walked to the "north" gate to proclaim it open. To the north lies a significant Sardis-type area and to the south lies a classic Sardis-type city. This prayer-walk to open the north gate, I believe, was a God-given strategy, partly to prevent the north gate being occupied by something else with false sight, such as a cult, and also strategic as the Jesus People Movement of the West Coast came in part to the San Francisco Bay area from the north. In due course the church will need to address both the issue of the arch and of the south gate.

The shutting down of true sight, then, is the primary work of the enemy. This was taking place in Philadelphia, so Jesus had to exhort them to "see." The challenge to sight was furthered increased by the internal situation. Jesus said that the church had "little power" (v. 8 NRSV), so the temptation to focus on their insignificance and simply to try and survive would have been strong. In the light of their little power the idea of an open door and the need to press through it with mission would have been somewhat of a challenge to their thinking. The only way to connect would be with true sight, with the eyes of faith – hence, the threefold exhortation to "see."

The second stronghold is a related one. We have already mentioned how Freemasons and Mormons are drawn to Philadelphia-type places, but also need to understand that these places are favored by cults of all types. Here Jesus expresses it by describing a *"synagogue of Satan"* (v. 9) that is making claims to being the true people of God. This is a claim that cults continually make, and again, as noted above, many times they will establish themselves in an entry place in the city.

An example of how the gates are occupied can be seen in a note I received from a pastor in another city in California that I recently visited. Although this city is significantly inland, it was a major port for sea-going trade. While there I taught on the nature of a gateway city. The pastor later wrote: "There are five Mormon churches in our city, all but one are on strategic entrances to the city and the fifth was on such a road but the city has grown around it. There are six Jehovah's-Witness churches; four are on strategic entrances to the city, two of which are only a few blocks away from the Mormons. All the other strategic entrances to the city have old time Pentecostal churches on them which at one time were the carriers of the Fire in the city."

In the letter the church in Philadelphia is promised that Satan's synagogue will come and bow down at their feet, acknowledging that the Lord has loved the church. This promise is dependent on the church seeing the open door and positioning themselves in the light of it. It seems the church is not called to focus so much on battling the cults, nor of establishing that they are right, but to so live that the favor of God becomes clear to those around. It is vital to establish truth – and we have read that to Philadelphia Jesus comes as the true one – but it will not be enough simply to establish truth at a cerebral level. The church is to keep focused on their call and be the means by which the gospel is released within and through the gateway city. Intimacy with the Lord is a major part of the warfare needed to break through so that the final testimony is concerning love not truth.

As with Smyrna (where there was also a synagogue of Satan) the church faces a significant battle in the realm of knowing it is legitimate. The nature of cults is that they claim legitimacy and make everything else legitimate. This battle can push the church toward an over-cautious and conservative position with no ability to take a risk, or conversely this can lead to one expression of church claiming God's approval over them – and by default God's disapproval over other expressions of the body of Christ.

The third stronghold here is found in the warning of Jesus who calls the church not to allow anyone to take away his or her crown. The type of crown mentioned here (*stephanos*) is the crown that the successful athlete who won the race would receive. Philadelphia as a city placed a high premium on its games, so this was a most apt description. The crown surely speaks of competing for the gates and also completing the task set before them. It is possible to get so far only for the crown to be snatched away. This represents a call from God for the church through warfare to establish on earth what Jesus has already declared; they must not only open the gate but they have to press right in to see that gate established at the level where no one can shut it.

The three central strongholds, then, are related together:

- the blindness that comes upon the church so that their calling and position is not discovered, with the result that (particularly in the gates)
- cults and false spiritual movements that promise sight and relationship with God flourish, with the consequence that deception is established and the seeing gift is stolen from the church. Once the church begins on the journey of recapturing the true calling on the city there has to be a perseverance, otherwise
- the church will not establish the gates to the place of openness and will find that their reward is stolen.

A promise of protection

In the midst of the letter Jesus makes a promise that those who "keep" hold of this word of endurance, will be "kept" from the hour of trial (v. 10). Although there is an eschatological element to this, the promise is given here in Philadelphia for them to experience in the here and now. There will be a major battle to open the gates and pressure will come on the city, and this same pressure will also seek to come on the church, but Jesus promises a protection on the church. Although the church in any given place is not totally exempt from the pressures around, another indication that a gateway place is breaking through would be when the church is not experiencing the same hardships that are on the city.

Jacob's dream

As I have already suggested, an Old Testament narrative that resonates with the Philadelphia situation would be Jacob's encounter with God at Bethel. As he sleeps, he dreams and then discovers that the place where he had slept was a gateway from earth to heaven. Like a number of gateway places Jacob was at a boundary, and there are those scholars who consider that the angels ascending were the ones that had been assigned to the previous territory, and the angels that were descending were the ones God was assigning to journey with Jacob into the new territory. He had safe passage from there, and his "going out and his coming in" was going to be protected. The open door for his journey, though, was because there was an open door from heaven to earth.

So gateway places have to create an opening from heaven to the earth in order to make effective openings on the earth. Once these openings are established there can be significant freedom of access for the angelic as part of the experience of such places.

To the overcomers

Jacob named the place "Bethel" – the house of God – and there is a promise to the overcomers that they will be part of the house (Temple) that God is building in that place. If Thyatira draws from the kingship imagery, and perhaps Sardis is reminiscent of the wisdom literature, then in Philadelphia there are allusions to the building of the Temple. In Philadelphia it was the custom for important citizens to have their names inscribed on pillars in the local temples, so the promise is particularly appropriate for this place. However, their names are not going to be written on some pillar in a pagan temple, but the people who hold through will be the actual pillars themselves that hold up what God is building, and they will receive the threefold name (*"the name of my God, and the name of the city of my God, the new Jerusalem, ... and my new name,"* v. 12) themselves.

There will be permanence about their position within the Temple and they will not be driven out of it through local circumstances. (This was a reference to the many who had decided to live outside the city due to dangers caused by the continuing earthquakes in the region.) The region might be difficult to live in and establish something in, but the promise from Jesus is that they will, indeed, be established. They will not be established for their own sake but with the knowledge that God is erecting a Temple – a dwelling place for His name – in their city. This Temple will, indeed, be a place of divine presence and of divine visitation but will also need to be a house of prayer for all nations.

The connection of a gateway (opening the doors for mission) and the establishment of the Temple is also reflected in Matthew's Gospel. Matthew's Gospel is full of the concept of the fulfillment of Scripture, both in terms of specific Old Testament Scriptures that are quoted, and also in the way it is written to convey the message of fulfillment of the whole of the Old Testament. In the opening verse Matthew lets us know that what we are going to read is "the book of the genealogy of Jesus Christ" (in Greek the book of the *genesis* of Jesus Christ), thus alerting us to the obvious allusion to the first book of the Old Testament. Jesus is set as the one who comes in fulfillment of the Old Testament Scriptures (he is the son of Abraham and of David). As the chapter continues, Matthew presents Jesus as the one who truly ends the Exile that "his people" have been experiencing because of their sin. He comes to save "his people" from their sins (1:21). He not only brings the people out of Exile but also brings them the presence of God, for He is called "Emmanuel" (1:23). In this first chapter, then, Jesus is presented as the one who is fulfilling the whole Old Testament destiny. In the final chapter the book ends with the well-known "Great Commission," but I suggest that there is more than a passing reference to what was (normally) the last book in the Jewish canon – the book of 2 Chronicles. In the closing verses of that book King Cyrus says that he has been given authority over the kingdoms of the earth and so he commissions those who are about to return to Jerusalem and rebuild the Temple, with the hope that the Lord will go with them (2 Chronicles 36:22–23). Jesus' claim at the end of Matthew's Gospel goes far beyond Cyrus' claim. There He says that all authority has been given to Him, that there has been a total "change of every guard," so to speak, and that (by inference) the Temple will be rebuilt, not in a specific place, but throughout the whole earth as nations are discipled. He also assures them that He will go with them (Matthew 28:18–20). The New Testament commission is for the disciples to go out through the gate and participate in the rebuilding of the Temple, so it is not surprising that it is at the gateway place that specific promises are made concerning the Temple.

So, in bringing this scripture from Matthew to bear on the gateway place, we can also suggest that discipling, commissioning and sending will be a major part of the gift to be released in gateway cities. These cities will prove to be strong places for mission training movements to be based, or for the churches to become strong mission sending bodies. There should be a strong expectation for the reality of God's presence among the believers in this type of city, and there should be released the dimension of the church as a house of prayer for all nations.

The second promise in this overcoming section is of the giving of a threefold name. The name of the Father, the new Jerusalem and Jesus' own new name will all be bestowed on them. The name giving indicates both ownership and identity. There will be no shame on the church, for there will be such an identification from heaven with these people. They truly will know that heaven has promised to be with them as they embrace their mission. Even the final destination (the new Jerusalem) will be written on them so they can have a strong confidence that, once their eyes have been opened to what Jesus has opened for them, heaven will gladly identify them as carrying the very seeds of the age to come. They will, indeed, be a city that is living experientially at an intersection between heaven and earth.

Final comments

Like all other places, gateway cities do not exist for themselves. The gate they open is to enable other places to release what they have. They have a particular relationship with the Sardis-type places (mercy/development) so that the well opened up there will have an outflow. They are promised a key which needs to be applied where they are, but the key released there will open many doors elsewhere. I also see a particular relationship with the final city that was written to, Laodicea. Although the church in Laodicea must open the door themselves, there are keys in Philadelphia that will enable shut doors to be swung wide open. Many gateway places are small, and many Laodicea-type places are rich and "important." Yet there is such a need for Laodicea-type places to break out of their independence and pride and receive help from what can be perceived as smaller and less important places.

So we call for the gateway places to open. We call for the gateway nations to rise to the challenge of leading the way with mission. We pray that gateway cities and nations will connect for the sake of the harvest. Come tell us what you see, tell us that the fields are white to harvest, that the door is open. We invite you to come; you are your key and you help our doors to open. Come tell us of heaven's resources that can take us to the next level.

Chapter 15

Laodicea: the Giving City

(Revelation 3:14–22)

Laodicea was one of the main banking centers for the ancient world and as such became a place of great wealth. In 60 AD the city was all-but destroyed in a violent earthquake, but unlike Philadelphia and Hierapolis, which were also affected, Laodicea did not want any financial aid from Rome to rebuild. The letter's statement concerning the church that it was rich and in need of nothing (v. 17) was an echo of what the city had said to Rome. Alongside the banking element there were two other resources that helped this city to develop wealth. It was known also for the soft, raven-black sheep's wool that eventually enabled the city to outstrip other garment manufacturers in the district, and there was a famous medical school that had in particular developed a compound for curing eye diseases called "Phrygian powder."

There are clear references to all the above within the letter, thus indicating that cities of this type perhaps have a greater propensity than others to squeeze the church into its own mould.

The well-known reference to the church being lukewarm is another clear allusion to the literal setting of the church. The city had grown very quickly but had one major problem. It did not have sufficient water to supply the city as a whole, so had to pipe in water from Denizili, some six miles to the south, via an aqueduct. The water was drawn from hot springs and did not have time to cool en route to Laodicea. The water also contained calcium carbonate deposits, so the net effect was that anyone who drank it would vomit it out. The church, Jesus is saying, is simply a reflection of the city, and He will vomit it out of His mouth if there is no change.

There is one other aspect about the lukewarm-ness of the water. In saying that they should have been either hot or cold there is almost certainly a reference to two other cities from the same region. Indeed, Laodicea made a tri-city formation along with Hierapolis, some six miles to the north, and with Colossae, some ten miles to the east. In Hierapolis there were famous hot springs that were frequented for their healing properties, whereas in Colossae there was the only supply of cold refreshing drinking water within the region. In using this illustration and by provocatively comparing Laodicea unfavorably to the two other (lesser) cities in the region, He is hitting at a major bondage – that of independence. Laodicea, like all other giving cities, desperately needs to recognize its need of help in order to release its destiny. Jesus certainly indicated that humility and dependence would be very necessary for the church to make progress in the city.

Jesus comes to a giving city

There is a cosmic dimension that surrounds the description of Jesus in this greeting: He is the Amen, the faithful and true witness, the beginning of God's creation. There is within the comment that Jesus is "the Amen" an allusion to Isaiah 65:16 where twice we read that God is *"the God of truth"* (Hebrew: the God of Amen). This leads to the promise of a new creation (65:17–25), which again fits so well here. Jesus is the faithful and true witness and the source (Greek: *arche*) of God's creation both in terms of the original creation and the new creation that is to come. He is the firstborn over all creation (Colossians 1:15–16).

Jesus is going to bring all of creation through to its appointed goal, of that we can be sure because He is the Amen. He will do so because He has been the faithful and true witness – there has been no deviation from the Messianic task entrusted to Him, and His faithfulness even led to His own death. This, though, qualifies Him as both source and Lord of all creation (*arche* can carry both senses).

Thus, He calls the church to receive Him in this way. They have first to receive Him as the Amen – as the final word. His challenge is, "Receive me without reservation, sign without even seeing the small print!"

Again applying the principle that how Jesus comes to a church is primarily what that church will have to reveal, we can understand from this that the Laodicean-type church is challenged to receive truth and to line up under it to the extent that there will be significant personal cost. However, this will enable the church to lay hold of the resources of creation at an incredible level.

A finishing gift

It is this reference to creation that enables us to suggest that there is a second complementary gift that will come forth in Laodicea-type places. Not only are they "giving" places but they also have a "finishing" gift. Ephesus, the city with the gift of beginnings, draws upon allusions from the Garden of Eden, the place of beginnings, but the final goal is not of going back to Eden but of all of creation being transformed. Christ comes to Laodicea as the one who was both the agent of creation and, through the cross, as the one by which all of creation will be restored. Laodicea, then, is called to bring out the resources of creation at an unprecedented level.

An element that is important to understand in finishing places is that the growth and development is not even. The growth is incremental and, as one aspect is released, the church is called to finish at each phase. As the transition point comes, there is the possibility of either birthing the work to a new level or of allowing a spirit of death to shut it down completely. Closely aligned to this spirit of death is a religious spirit.

Some central characteristics

Giving/finishing cities will generally have some or all of the following characteristics:

- a strong financial element, drawing to itself financial institutions such as banking, insurance and the like that deal directly with the economics of that society
- it will normally have been founded on a strong trading basis even when there were few natural reasons for a community to grow up in that location
- a strong medical presence (Pergamum-type places too will have this element).

Surface strongholds

One of the cities I travel to in Europe is a giving city and, indeed, it is the capital city of a nation with the same gifting. The city has within it two locations where there has been a significant level of bloodshed. On one location stands the headquarters of the national bank and on the other is situated the national stock market. In the book *Gaining Ground* I explain how bloodshed is one of the primary means by which land is polluted and how such pollution opens a place up to demonic strongholds. So, given that bloodshed attracts the demonic, it is clear that the enemy has sought to build up a significant bondage over these two very influential economic institutions. If the enemy can lock up the finances of the city, then it is easy to see how this will be a primary place where the battle will be focused. Hence, in such places whenever the church is not generous with its finances, or is continually in a place of lack, we can easily conclude that there are significant levels of stronghold present.

There seems to me, then, to be three immediate areas where it can be easy to see the level of bondage. A lack of generosity by the church, as indicated above, is an obvious sign, as also is the experience within the church of continual lack. The third area, I would suggest, is drawn from the complementary finishing gift.

When there is a history in the city of not finishing what has begun, we can quickly conclude that the church has much work to do to get her breakthrough.

Enemy strategies

In the letter there are a number of enemy strategies that Jesus exposes, and it would appear that this type of city strongly seeks to shape the church in its own image. Jesus speaks of independence, blindness and a corresponding unwillingness to be self-critical, and a lack of zeal. Running in and through all of the above is a propensity to succumb to a religious spirit with the church being reduced to being a religious version of the city. We have already noted two ways in which the city has shaped the church in connection with the letter's references to the water supply and the need to purchase true eye-salve. The shaping of the church by the city will always result in the church becoming a religious institution, rather than the Body of Christ that seeks to be redemptive in and through every sphere. The religious spirit is also personified by the term "I" (so we read in this letter that the church was saying, *"I am rich; I have acquired wealth ... "*, v. 17). Christ is no longer at the center but the church is in the process of displacing Him. This is religion, where it is all about the church and the Savior is sidelined.

These cities and the churches present in these cities have a default mode of falling into independence. This will manifest itself in the city being independent from other cities, particularly by giving off a signal of being superior to other places, and by one congregation standing aloof from another one in the same city. In one such city I can remember addressing the pastors who gathered together with the following challenge. I told them that their city was a prime place for a new church to be planted. Someone could, I suggested, come in and begin a new church. Various people would leave the existing churches, providing the leader of the new plant with a core of some fifty or so people to start with. Due to the wealth within the city, that church planter would have sufficient finance to live off and would be happy with his new congregation. I informed these existing pastors that this was the scenario they were inviting to happen. Although they would not be happy with such an outcome, I suggested that they were actually inviting it, for as long as they lived in independence from each other they were "inviting" independence to come in through the gates.

For a significant breakthrough to take place in such a city, its congregations must be willing to express their need of other expressions of the Body of Christ. Independence can have no part in the DNA of the church in those cities. The church has to develop something of an opposite spirit, and I suggest that there has to be a positive honoring of other expressions of church. There has to be a celebration of the diversity.

Beyond that those city leaders need to be ready to welcome input from the outside. The "we have no need of help" spirit has to be broken. So, not only do those cities need to be willing to give without strings attached, they must also be ready to receive. Paul, writing to Philippi – another giving city – said they had entered into partnership with him in *"giving and receiving"* (Philippians 4:15).

Jesus rebukes the church in Laodicea, stating that it was blind and as a result made false statements about itself. The blindness here is not a lack of vision, but an inability to see itself self-critically. This is the blindness that pride brings about. Jesus calls for a recognition of the sorry state of affairs, and calls the church to respond by asking Him for true wealth, clean garments and true eye ointment. There is no way forward in these cities without humble repentance. The wealth Jesus offers has to be purchased; the gold on offer is gold that has come through the fire. Both of these descriptions suggest that there will be no progress without embracing suffering. Breaking through in these cities will be costly, and the cost will often be in literal material terms. Sacrificial giving will be required in order to gain authority for a breakthrough.

There is clothing that must be received to cover their shame. Again there is a strong inference here of repentance and self-awareness that is required. They cannot hide behind a façade but have to acknowledge that they have not done well and without the clothing of Christ they are shamefully naked.

Undergirding the above two issues there has to be a crying out to see themselves self-critically. The cry is not first of all to receive vision for the future, but for self-awareness in the present.

Zeal has to replace lukewarmness. The spirit of complacency is another major bondage over these types of cities. These cities have a key part to play in bringing to completeness the work of God in an area, and the enemy will keenly resist their breakthrough. Only those with a zeal and passion will be able to harness the wealth of the city for the sake of the work of the Kingdom.

When giving cities break through, they uncover amazing gifts. There is true wealth to come forth that will manifest itself not just in material aid but also through the gift of people. The people will come with a strong gift of perseverance for they will carry that finishing anointing to bring many situations to a completion. The enemy loves to keep these places in independence for, when they are released and release their gift at the right time, they will prove to be key to helping many other places to complete what God has given them to do. This is certainly true in the Laodicea-type of cities.

Philippi – breakthrough for the city

Philippi is another city that I believe carries the same gift as Laodicea. I have already mentioned that an indication of this is that the Philippian believers had partnered with Paul in both giving and receiving. It is interesting to note how Paul came to the city of Philippi in Acts. Although I am not suggesting that there is only one way that such a city can be impacted, there were some clear steps that Paul followed.

First, he went looking for those who were in prayer (Acts 16:13). There has to be a birthing of strategy in prayer for these places as the independence and supposed ability to make it through their own abilities is so high.

In the place of prayer Paul was able to share the gospel and his heart, with the result that the Lord opened the heart of Lydia. She was involved in business, and it is usually vital to find an inroad into the business community in these cities. From there the gospel spread to her household. In this type of city we must think outside the box, as the religious spirit is very quick to push us back in the box of predictability.

After this initial breakthrough Paul continued with the practice of going to the place of prayer. Again this continual habit is a significant key. The next impact is at so many levels. A child is impacted – in these cities it is vital to reach children. The sophistication of "we have it all" is often broken open through the offence of the simplicity of children. A demon is impacted, but this spirit of false prophecy is more than just a demon as it in some ways relates to spiritual powers over the area, and the work of this demon was also tied into the economic structures of the city.

Now something truly is moving, and there is a reaction against Paul and Silas, but the end result is the birth of a work of God and the shaking of both the heavenly and the earthly powers in the city.

As I say, this is not a blueprint, but I believe, in the light of the pride of the city, it does show us some significant elements. Those elements are: prayer, business, children, and power encounters that hit at the heart of the structures.

All the above elements undermine the arrogance, independence and supposed wealth of the city, and all are bathed in prayer. These cities can break through, but only if the powers are confronted. Of all the cities the battle is perhaps the most severe here as to whether the church will shape the city, or the city will make the church into its own image.

Finally – counsel released

Jesus has told the city of Laodicea, *"I reprove and discipline those whom I love"* (v. 19 NRSV). These are words that recall the Old Testament scripture that God is a father who must discipline His children (Proverbs 3:11–12). So part of the release here is of knowing the fatherhood of God. As Father He is the one who is willing to confront us in order to make us ready to receive our inheritance.

The promises that are granted to Laodicea are dependent on responding to the knock at the door. Jesus requests entrance in order to be intimate with His people. He wishes to eat with them, but the meal that is described is the one at the end of the day. All work and activity are over, there are no time restraints. So the call from Jesus is to welcome Him in as a lover (reminiscent of Song of Songs 5:2) and for there to be intimacy. In a major financial center, where independence and self-sufficiency wish to rule, the key to breakthrough is to submit to the discipline of the Father and to enter into intimacy with Christ.

It is from intimacy, and only from a place of intimacy, that the promise of rule opens up. This is not about an exercise of authoritarian rule: it is from the place of intimacy that counsel comes as hearts are shared, and from there that the counsel of the Lord can then be released.

This means that a giving place, when it breaks free from its independence and pride and comes to live in an intimate relationship with the Lord, will become a place where strategies will be revealed. However, the Lord will only reveal those once the other issues are dealt with. Nevertheless, this is one of the gifts that such a city or nation has to offer. The pathway is one of humility, but the release is just what we need, for there are so many places that have started well that will need the finishing cities and nations to come through to enable them to complete the task the Lord has set before them.

So we call you, with all that God has graced you with, to open up to Him. We declare that, if you will open up to Him, He will come to you with His presence. He will give you all the time you need and will grace you with divine counsel. We say that we need you; it is not your wealth that we seek, but the grace that is on you from heaven. Open yourself up to the Lord; be open with others; be ready to give and to receive. There is a journey that you need to go on, and there are companions that need you so desperately.

Postscript

In writing this book with Mike and Sue, my prayer is that the church in whatever city or region it finds itself planted by the Lord will find fresh inspiration to reach out for the appropriate strategy for its situation. The work before us is enormous, but surely not to the scale that the early church faced. Twelve core disciples, 120 in an upper room, and something like 12 per cent of the entire Roman Empire as committed disciples within 300 years. This works out to be a growth rate of some 40 per cent per decade every decade. They actually believed that the commission from heaven and the breath of the Spirit constituted them as the Body of Christ. They had the conviction that through the resurrection Jesus filled *"everything in every way"* (Ephesians 1:23) and that they, as the Body of Christ, were to grow to the fullness of the stature of this Christ (Ephesians 4:13).

If we could recapture some of their enthusiasm, some of their infectious faith, and perhaps their sense of adventure I wonder what might take place. In my context, the continent of Europe, I am asking what would take place if we made that all-out response to the call from heaven for Jesus to have His church back. I am painfully aware that it might mean the end of some forms of church, but the possibility of participating in the life of God pulsating through the Body of Christ would be a reward beyond anything we deserve.

I trust that the material we have presented will stimulate your imagination and cause you to go back again to Scripture in order for your biblical vision for your situation to be strengthened.

In closing I note below a few areas that I have discovered about traveling safely from place to place. I include this, as there is an increasing call on the Body of Christ to be mobile, to cross over boundaries and to go and help others. I believe that the Lord wants to watch over our going out and our coming in, to bless our exits and entrances. Following on from the issue of entrances and exits I include a few comments on safety during seasons of specific spiritual warfare.

Sending and receiving

If we are to fulfill our desires to see whole cities and regions impacted, then we will need to embrace the need for partnership wholeheartedly. This will include partnerships within the city as we seek to embody the concept of the church in the locality. It will also include partnerships with those divine connections from outside the city. God will join to the city those who carry apostolic, prophetic and evangelistic gifting. In the past many prophets and apostles have only worked with churches of their own denomination or stream; now it is time to see apostolic and prophetic ministry that is released to the city as a whole. It would be wonderful to have, for example, an apostle who is from a Methodist denomination working in a city where there was no lively Methodist church. In other words, we need to see cities connect with those who are carrying the specific grace to help them break through as a city.

God-given connections are so necessary. Twice the Old Testament Scriptures indicate that in a God-initiated partnership we can expect to see significant increases (Leviticus 26:8 and Deuteronomy 32:30). It was the partnering of those who were willing to be mobile with those who were prepared to fight for their land that was the key to taking the Promised Land. I am referring to Numbers 32 where we read that Moses exhorted the tribes to the east of the Jordan to cross over the river to help the other tribes gain their land.

This scripture has been a key that has shaped up many who have traveled to help cities and regions break through. It is vital that there are people in place who are saying that they are there for the "long haul," willing to pay the price of seeing their region impacted. They are increasing in authority, for in saying that this is "their place" they are taking responsibility for what happens there. It is also important that these people find the connections with those who are willing to travel and cross over boundaries with no other agenda than to help. These people must come with empty hands, knowing that whatever they carry they received freely, and so must give it away without cost.

Giving and receiving help is what we are called to. To be effective in this, an understanding of the nature of being sent and being received are therefore very important factors.

The Holy Spirit loves to lead people to cross boundaries. The book of Acts is full of this aspect. It is about a people being sent and about a people and their message being received.

Entries and exits

Over the past few years as I have worked into cities, I have become very aware of the need for right entries and also of right exits. These issues become increasingly critical if our agenda is an offensive one, in the sense of taking territory strategically from the enemy. I cannot claim to understand all the factors involved but have become convinced that when the entry is wrong we become very vulnerable to the attacks of the enemy. There are casualties in every war, and despite the fact that Jesus did not promise us a safe existence, we should seek to keep all casualties to a minimum. One way in which this can be minimized is through making a right entry.

Those who live in a place have an authority that those who travel in do not have. They have this authority simply because they have made a commitment to that place as a result of God's call on their lives to live there. There is always sufficient grace to do whatever the Lord asks us to do, so those people have a grace on their lives that is related to their call. When people travel in, they cannot come with that authority or grace. However, they do come with another type of authority. When He sent out His

disciples, Jesus said that, wherever they were received as sent
from Him, the people would in fact receive Him (Matthew 10:40;
Luke 10:16). That is an awesome statement and means that,
whenever there are those who travel, they need to know that
Jesus has indeed sent them at that time to that place.

Here, then, are a number of perspectives on making a good
entry:

▶ *Be convinced that the time and place is right.*
If we travel we should not simply accept invitations because our
schedule is clear. We need to be in the habit of praying over
our calendars so that, when invites come our way, we know that
it is prayer that has released the invites and we can quickly
discern if they fit within the burden that God has been giving us
in the times of prayer.

▶ *When making an entrance come in a spirit of humility.*
When entering look to flow with what God has been doing and
saying in that place. There is a limit as to what can be brought,
but there is a tremendous amount that can be accelerated
through those who travel.

▶ *Unite, but don't confuse, the two types of authority.*
We need to recognize that those who are resident have an authority within their geography. Those who travel have an authority
that comes from being sent, and as the two types of authority are
combined there is an increased effectiveness. Those in a place
need to welcome those who have come so that there is a covering
over them, but the same needs to be done in reverse. Many times
the local people come under increased pressure and even sickness
when the time approaches for a team to arrive. It is the arriving
team that has an authority through being sent by the Lord to
extend a covering over the people. I learned through a painful
experience to extend the boundary of covering as wide as possible
and as soon as possible (and by this I mean even before arriving in
the geography). In one city to which we traveled, there had been a
number of freak accidents that had happened to the children of

those in the church. We shut that down in prayer, and the accidents stopped. However, the accidents then began to happen to those who were not believers but were employed by believers. We also shut that down, but then the accidents spread almost immediately to the children of those employees. This eventually went as far as one young girl being seriously injured on one of the oldest crossroads in Europe on the day after we had prayed there. It was a painful lesson, for I believe we could have saved that young girl and her family their ordeal. We should have set the boundary much wider than we did, and not just in response to what was taking place.

I suggest the following aspects will help in making a good exit:

▶ *Break off the "junk" from the city before you leave.*
I have heard so many stories of how a team has had a tremendous impact in a place, but on the day before they left for home, or since they had come home, team members had become sick and not been able to shake it off. I believe that there is a grace to live with junk when one is called to live in a place. There will be grace to cover a person who is called to go there and work, but, once they leave that geography, they will not receive the same level of grace to deal with any junk they take with them. The grace is for the geography. It is vital, then, that (like the disciples) the dust is shaken from our feet as we leave. It can be good to have local people pray for a safe exit and to pray a release from whatever contamination has come. If it is taken from that place, it will be harder to shift when in another geography.

At the end of one year, while in Hannover on a prophetic conference, one of those leading the conference suggested that those who traveled regularly should be prayed for, to remove any contamination through our travels over the year. I was more than happy to submit to prayer, but my expectation was not too high. I was stunned, though, at the results. Immediately it was if a physical weight left me.

Particularly if a person has been unable to shake a sickness which he or she has suffered since traveling to a specific place, it will be very important to address the connection with that place and to break the wrong connection. Sometimes it might even be advantageous to get someone from that place to do that for them. Better still, of course, is to have it done before one leaves the geography.

▶ *Know what to carry and what to leave behind.*
God will release burdens when a person travels, but it is important to discover which of the burdens God has released he or she is to continue to carry and which were for the time while there. Again there is grace to carry God-given burdens.

In this issue of exiting, it can be a good practice to break bread together with those who are resident in that place. In this way we are affirming our commitment and covenant together.

Safety in warfare

There are certain horror stories that can be told about how people have suffered through being involved in certain aspects of spiritual warfare. (It is also true that many people have been involved in the same supposed "dangerous" practices but have suffered no ill effects.) My own opinion is that it is not normally as simple as forbidding certain practices but that, with a little bit of wisdom being exercised, personal damage can be minimized – I also have to acknowledge that in warfare there are casualties. We are in warfare and the enemy seeks to damage us as much as possible.

Here, then, are some aspects that are wisely put in place:

▶ *Live in relational wholeness.*
Or to put this in Pauline language, *"as far as it depends on you, live at peace with everyone"* (Romans 12:18). In certain circumstances full reconciliation is beyond our control, but we are to do everything within our power to promote peace. By so doing we shut down opportunities for the enemy to come and damage us.

If there are damaged relationships that we can repair, it is most unwise to be involved in strategic warfare.

▶ *Have humility as a covering.*
We are told to humble ourselves (James 4:6–10) and to clothe ourselves with humility toward one another (1 Peter 5:5–9), and in both of those scriptures we find that the context is one of confrontation with the devil. (By the way we are not told to ignore the devil but to actively resist him.) I am convinced that the clothing of humility acts like a cloaking device that renders us all-but invisible to the enemy's camp. The devil is clothed with pride and it is those who come in the spirit of humility, knowing that they are following in the steps of the one who humbled Himself even to the point of death on a cross, that can safely make advances into territory that the enemy has sought to occupy.

▶ *Pray for those over you in the Lord.*
In the Kingdom we are not to lord it over one another; yet we should be able to recognize that there are those whom the Lord has placed over us for our protection and release. A good principle is to pray for those who are in that position, for by so doing we are actually praying for all who are under them (and that includes us!). I suggest that, when Paul instructs Timothy to pray for everyone (1 Timothy 2:1–4), one of the means by which we do so is by praying for those in authority. If they are vulnerable spiritually, so are the people for whom God has appointed them, and conversely if they are prayed for, so are the people that they carry responsibility for. Consequently, one of the quickest ways to obtain a covering from the Lord is by praying for those that we know are over us in Him (and by the way this does not mean that we have to agree with everything they believe or teach).

So, finally two comments. First, there are two main reasons why I have deliberately tried not to make too many comments about specific places in the book: my desire to protect those places from wrong exposure, and to avoid categorizing cities and nations prematurely. I intend to use the web site www.wild-fire.co.uk as a place where categorizations and comments can be made – and also changed and updated!

Second, I submit this book to you, the readers, as those who have a desire for Jesus to manifest Himself in our cities and nations. If there is material in this book that helps you break through in your situation, my prayer is that you will feel free to implement it as you see fit. No doubt, as you do so, you will improve on what is within these pages. We are in partnership together for the sake of the gospel and, if the Lord will help us and if we will humble ourselves to work together, we can expect a new day – even a new day in my continent of Europe.

Appendix 1

Stories from Those in the Dispersed Church

It was suggested that I (Mike) write something about people calling for the ministry gifts to serve them in their place of work. As I did not feel qualified to do that, I have asked some people to tell their stories. These are people who see their work as the place God has called them to and have thought about how they and people like them can be equipped.

▶ *James Fathers is a Senior Lecturer in Product Design. He is also involved in a doctoral research project investigating the role of design education in the context of developing countries as well as consultancy on maximizing creativity. He lives in Cardiff with wife Kath and two young sons, David and Nathan.*

In what follows I am reflecting a selection of the questions and responses I have asked and been asked on my journey.

Why is it so hard to explain? I'm so tired of spending twenty minutes explaining why and what I am doing just to get people on the same page – or more correctly to get people to understand the page I am on.

A big issue for those who have chosen to be outside of traditional church expressions is how to get support. Although there are no easy answers, relationships are the key, and I suggest finding at least one person who can share the joys and frustrations. Prayer triplets might work, but generally meetings are not the way forward. I give a big "yes" to gatherings of like-minded individuals, each with passion, direction, hopes, dreams and frustrations. As one bard recently said, "The meetings are over, the gatherings have begun ..."

How about, though, exploring church with the unchurched? I have recently helped facilitate a semi-regular informal meeting of a group of students interested in social justice and design who want to do more than talk about it. This has sprung from some design projects within the curriculum, which focus on areas of design, and have been inspired by my journey of discovery to find the Kingdom of God as expressed by design. The group comprises an eclectic mix of people who want to make a difference. I suggest that this could even be a (subconscious) mentoring of young people in the values of the Kingdom before they are introduced to the King.

Where else are Kingdom values being explored? Probably everywhere! In films, books and song. For the cry of creation, especially the frustration of creation as found in Romans 8, is expressed in a vast number of creative outlets.

Where does worship fit? Worship – that place of relocation and gaining perspective that is so vital in all of our spiritual lives, yet so hard to find outside of an institutional church construct. Again groups of friends seem to be one answer, particularly where we meet across boundaries of tradition because of a mutual need.

Where does the "spiritual" fit in the day to day of work? The reality lies somewhere in between daily quiet times and the dislocation of the Sunday meeting. Again relationship is the key where true friends are journeyed with who stick through the hard times and love blindly through times of misunderstanding and backlash.

I have found that, as soon as one stops skating across the surface and begins to own and care for the place of influence God has given, the thorns and thistles of opposition will be encountered. The key is to bless and carry on creating, digging and calling for new shapes and expressions of Jesus people in the landscape.

In giving some small pieces of advice to those asking where to start, I suggest that you have to follow your heart's desires, so discovering what you really want to do. Perhaps ask, what have you always dreamed of doing? That gives you a start point and then the journey begins. From there the choice is of being a tourist or a pilgrim. Are you really going to spend some time finding out how best to do this thing?

Knowing which way to go is a challenge, but my experience is often a case of following the trail of grace appointments and unexpected blessings. Following one's heart desires is often a surfing exercise, going with the flow, holding things lightly and pushing doors to see which of them open. A trail of blessings and grace as you follow your heart desires in finding and digging that "seam" which yields a regular stream of grace surprises – especially when it seems everything else has dried up.

▶ *Andrew Winter is the director of Source, an advertising agency in Deptford, South East London. A Director of the Lewisham Chamber of Commerce, he gives his time to support several organizations at board level, including A Glimmer of Hope, Common Purpose, Get Set for Citizenship SRB Programme, the McMillan Legacy Group and Fountain Gate Christian Community. He is thirty-one years old, married with two children and a member of The Bear church, which meets in a pub on Deptford High Street.*

I am struggling with this one as I have felt a little deserted by previous churchy people on this journey into using creativity to transform my community through business. I started *Source* as an advertising agency four years ago and at that time both MY and ML as my pastors were instrumental in encouraging me to launch out into starting the business. Both gave me a theological framework for the instinct that was driving me: God's passionate plan to shake His creativity out of the churches and into environments where most people spend their time and energies – the spheres of work. But since I made that jump into hyperspace and M left our church, not too many others filled their shoes! I'm not moaning that I haven't had the support; it's just the effect is you become isolated and doubt your motivations. Suddenly you're in the pursuit of selfish ambition rather than holy Kingdom building.

Funnily enough, the best support has come from mates who run other Christian businesses. CH runs a landscaping business and we have given loads of mutual encouragement, usually over lunch or breakfast. When you pursue excellence in any field, those around you often suffer – family, kids, and friendship. It's the cost of dedication. It is so good to have an empathetic mate to laugh at the conflict situations and to pray for breakthrough financially in the business and to help you lift your eyes to the bigger picture of Jesus working in the cities, through businesses, through relationships, through people. Without a mate like C I'm sure I would have been tempted to jack it all in long ago and opt for an easier route to provide for my family that was more 9 to 5.

If I did it all over again I would set up a business board of people that understood the spiritual significance of Christians in local business and could provide the prayer support necessary for the fight – in the same way as a youth project is prayed and supported and governed by a management committee – wise elders and pioneering creative youngsters to direct God's light and understanding on my path and that of my staff.

▶ *Kate McKinley lives near Yeovil and is married to Paul, an engineer. She runs a PR and marketing consultancy called Shout and initiates gatherings for people with a passion and vision for their work.*

It sometimes seems like God's working people and those gifted with the specific ministries set out in Ephesians 4 have got used to living without each other. We appear, on the whole, to live separate lives, so maybe it's no surprise the Body of Christ isn't being built up and unified as much as it could or should. Whatever the reason for this separateness – and it's probably got a lot to do with the divided world view that's blinded us – now feels like a good time to begin to close the gap! In fact, if the knowledge of the glory of the Lord is to cover the earth, we absolutely must.

The book of Acts is a great place to check out how working saints and ministry-gift people partnered together and, with a growing hunch that now is the time to be digging for more understanding, I've started to explore Acts with fresh eyes.

Imagine, for example, the consequences if Peter hadn't responded to the call from a working saint – Cornelius, a high-ranking army officer? If that partnership hadn't come together, the Holy Spirit might never have come to the Gentiles. And in reading through Acts it's clear that working people and ministry-gift people kind of hung out together. They stayed in each other's homes; they ate together. They were friends.

Could it be that today there is a whole bunch of lonely ministry-gifted people and another bunch of saints feeling isolated? In my experience, we've not been great on the friendship stakes with each other.

But in these wonderful, adventurous and scary days, we must rediscover friendship with each other because it is a powerful partnering. What's held us back from this partnering? From conversations with friends, I've sensed a reluctance to seek out that equipping for fear of being controlled, taken over and suddenly finding the good works many are doing have become a church project. There is also some confusion over what exactly the descriptive names given in Ephesians 4 really mean. Maybe we've either misused or overused the terms "apostles," "prophets," etc., and in doing so weakened them in some way. But as many are discovering their work – paid or unpaid – to be the call of God on their lives, the need for equipping is real and urgent.

So, as a working saint running a business, why do I want the ministry gifts and what will that partnering look like in action? As I've begun to explore, there are a couple of things I've observed and a story to tell which has encouraged me so much.

First, the story. For a number of months the business I run hit a cash flow crisis caused by late-paying clients resulting in the usual letters from the bank. I happened to mention the situation to a friend of mine. Now I'm not sure either my friend or I would describe him as an "apostle" although he does, in my view, have an apostolic gifting. However, he's first and foremost my friend. I also know he is committed to supporting and serving into the lives of working people like me. He himself is not in paid employment. My friend offered to collect my business debts. Within days the money came in. God reminded me of this when, a couple of months later, an even worse cash crisis hit. As my husband and I prayed, God reminded us about the help our friend had been and urged us to call for help again. We did. Our friend immediately said yes, although interestingly when he rang the late-paying clients, they all told him the money had already been sent. By the end of that week the business was owed nothing and was back in the black.

I learnt a lot from that crisis time. Firstly, there are times when a particular situation in a work setting needs a definite shift, breakthrough or revelation – that's when I'd want to call in a ministry-gift person! Our friend brought that blessing and break-through.

I also realized God is really wanting to link people, to close the gap between working people and ministry-gift people and cut through the isolation and loneliness. His links are for friendship and to bring about change and shifts when they're needed. We were also able to bless my friend by paying him some money (not that he asked for it), so the blessing cuts both ways.

The other thing I've noticed is that the generation of young apostles, prophets, etc., often seem to quite naturally respond to the needs of the saints. It's as if it's in their spiritual genes and they absolutely know it's part of what they're meant to do – and they do so with no agendas, usually outside church struc-tures in very informal ways and with utter humility. But whether the ministry-gift people are in their twenties or sixties, I don't care. As one of God's working people I'm learning to call for equipping and help more than I've ever done. There is so much you can help and equip us with, and it's time to rediscover how together we can do this – oh, and be friends!

Appendix 2

Summary Table
of the Seven Churches

By way of summary, on the following pages I enclose a table of the seven churches and how they can work together in aligning themselves with the New Jerusalem that comes down from heaven to earth.

The New Jerusalem

Type	First: Ephesus	Facilitate: Smyrna	Establish: Pergamum	Develop: Sardis	Gateway: Philadelphia	Finish: Laodicea
Greeting	7 angels and 7 lamps	First and last; the one who is alive	Two-edged sword	7 angels and 7 spirits	Key of David	Faithful witness and beginning of creation
Purpose	Destiny of whole church	Can complete, in spite of pressure	Warfare is needed	A resource for the whole church with enough supply	Open doors that cannot be shut	Resources from heaven and earth to complete the task
Calling	To birth new things and be clear for the whole church	To be responsive and so facilitate what is new; to experience God's deliverance	To establish what has been birthed	To develop what has been birthed and be a supply for the whole Body	To keep the door of mission open	To be a giving city and thus supply both heavenly and earthly resources
Issues	False apostolic; hierarchy; simply project orientated	Faith to complete; yielding to the pressures	Passivity, compromise and control	Past reputation; not completing; sleep	Blindness and cults	Pride; independence; blindness

Key to success	Permission for new	Richness and priorities	Warfare	Who they are: identity	Sight	Counsel and resource
Part to play	Bring the new: innovation	Responding to the new and gently provoking the establishing places, in spite of pressure	Opening to the prophetic, embracing warfare – otherwise they dwell in the wilderness	Drawing other places through/ giving ample provision through a developing gift	Responding to what is being developed/ standing in a place of sight for the release of mission	Being willing to receive help, so that there is a release of resources for what has begun to be completed

Model: Thyatira

Eyes of fire: sight pervades everything that takes place so that nothing is hidden

Feet of fire: the feet will tread on the works of the enemy and bring good news to all that God reigns over all

Jezebel: every false form of authority will be challenged

Rule the nations: the true calling of the Body of Christ will be released in all its diversity

If you have enjoyed this book and would like to help us to send a copy of it and many other titles to needy pastors in the **Third World**, please write for further information or send your gift to:

Sovereign World Trust
PO Box 777, Tonbridge
Kent TN11 0ZS
United Kingdom

or to the '**Sovereign World**' distributor in your country.

Visit our website at **www.sovereign-world.org**
for a full range of Sovereign World books.